MANAGING AND MARKETING YOUR WEBSITE

Jim Hutchinson

Oak Tree Press

Dublin

Oak Tree Press
Merrion Building
Lower Merrion Street
Dublin 2, Ireland
www.oaktreepress.com

A catalogue record of this book is
available from the British Library.

ISBN 1-86076-124-0

Printed in Ireland by Colour Books Ltd.

ABOUT THE AUTHOR

Jim Hutchinson is Managing Director of Arctic Advertising, a Dublin-based interactive promotions agency. Arctic specialises in the management and marketing of websites. As an ex-pat Canadian residing in Dublin, he has worked with Irish web houses and ISPs throughout the early stage of Internet development in Ireland. After graduating in communication arts/journalism at Durham College, Oshawa, Ontario, in 1987, he became interested in the Internet as a research tool in helping him in his role as finance editor for Canadian Press, Canada's national news agency.

CONTENTS

Chapter 4

Chapter 5

Chapter 6

Chapter 7

Chapter 8

FIGURES

ACKNOWLEDGEMENTS

I would like to thank all of the people and corporations who took part in the case studies and provided insights into the running of their websites.

An especially big thank you to Edel Cheasty for all her support and encouragement; without it, this book would never have seen the light of day. A special mention goes to friends and family back home in Canada for all their support and encouragement throughout my career.

1

INTRODUCTION

Congratulations! Your website has just gone, or is about to go live online. A job well done — time to relax and rest on the laurels, right? Wrong! Now the real work begins. The site must be managed, marketing, promoted and developed on an ongoing basis if it's to be successful.

The only way to make a website successful is to spend time and money promoting and marketing it. You can either handle this work yourself, appoint someone within the organisation to do it, or outsource it to a specialist company. This book has been designed to help you understand the amount of time, effort and money that should be spent to create a successful website.

In this publication we'll look at:

- **Content**: Why there is no substitute for high quality content.

- **Search Engines**: What they are, how they work and why they're the first step in promoting your site.

- **Publicity**: How to generate it and use it wisely, and why without it your website will never get any traffic.

- **Media Planning and Buying**: Looking to buy space for your site? Or maybe you are planning to sell space? We'll examine the ins and outs, the jargon and how to devise a strategic media plan.

- **Results**: How to read the results of your marketing and advertising campaigns to find out if you have a successful website.

- **Site Management**: Why your site must change and how to find and review the latest technology on the web.

- **Case Studies**: The best way to learn is from other people's successes and mistakes. In this chapter we'll look at other sites — some successful, some less so — and note the ideas to follow and the mistakes to avoid.

- **Glossary of terms**: Want to know what all that jargon means? Just look here and hopefully it will all become clear.

People often ask how much money they should spend on marketing and promoting their site. Simple: it's recommended that you spend at the least the same amount on marketing and promoting the site as you did creating it and — if you can afford it — even more. After all, like any product, sites must be managed and promoted to be successful. Many people look for some secret or "holy grail" to make their website successful. There is no secret way or shortcut that can bring you overnight success. The only way to ensure traffic to your site is hard work and diligence. It means registering and monitoring placement with search engines; long hours spent surfing the Internet to develop affinity marketing and promotional links with related but non-competitive websites; writing and distributing press releases to online and traditional publications and news outlets; developing a budget for web-based advertising . . . In short, you only get out of your website what you put into it.

Many organisations wrongly believe that once the site has been constructed and registered with a few search engines, the work is done and the hits will then roll in. Nothing could be further from the truth. To succeed with your site, you must work on it as much as possible. For some businesses, this means hiring an extra employee as a webmaster; for others, it may involve appointing someone within the organisation to monitor and market the website. And for a very small company, it may well be the managing director who takes on this responsibility. However, this responsibility must be accepted by someone in order to have a successful site.

To create a successful site you must:

- Update the content frequently;

- Monitor search engine placement and re-register when necessary;

- Research and contact related but non-competitive sites about exchanging links;

- Examine the potential of buying online advertising space;

- Develop and maintain an online publicity campaign;

- Monitor and data-mine visitor information and optimise your site from these results.

Having a website is easy. Having a successful website is a lot of hard work. However, you are now on the right track towards developing a site that people will want to visit and revisit.

US multinational Procter & Gamble has allocated over $3 million for Internet marketing and promotion. Site advertising budgets of over $100,000 are not unheard of. While Europe still appears to lag behind the US in moving with the web, many companies, and Irish ones in particular, are increasingly aware of the opportunities offered by a well-managed website.

Some of the more successfully managed sites in Ireland include *The Irish Times*, Guinness, Go Ireland, *The Irish Independent*, The Virtual Pub, and many others. This book will look at why they're successful and what goes into making their sites attractive to readers.

2

CONTENT — THE ELVIS FACTOR

Content is King! This can never be stressed enough. There is no substitute for high quality, well-constructed content. This is something you can't cheat or cut corners on if you want a successful website.

A simple definition of content is anything that appears on your web page. This includes graphics, images, text, computer programs, etc. The secret in dealing with content is not only how it's developed, but also how it's used.

When developing a website, too many people believe the old axiom "more is better". Following this advice will do far more harm than good in creating a successful site. In the beginning of web development, sites gave out so much information that people became confused and the message became scrambled and often ignored.

Many people wonder why their site has not been successful. They go on to say that the site uses the latest technology, all the latest Internet bells and whistles, that they've even registered with search engines, but still no one comes. The answer to these problems can be obtained by clearly answering the following three questions:

1. Why should someone visit your website in the first place?

2. What makes your site different from those of your competitors?

3. Why should people return to the site on a regular basis?

The answer to all these questions is the same: *Content.*

Why should someone visit your site? To receive high quality, informative material on your product or service, which only you can make available. Why are you different from your competitors? Simple: you offer better and more attractive content and information on your organisation. And if you provide up-to-date information, people will return to the website on a regular basis. After all, isn't that what creating a successful website is all about — to bring people in and sell them your product or service? Well you can't sell to them if you can't bring them in, and you can't bring them in without high quality content.

Content is important not only for the information you provide to your audience, but also for search engine registration and ranking. When a search engine is asked to look for keywords in its database of sites, it looks for how many times and where the keywords are located in the body copy (editorial) of the site. The more times, and higher up, they appear in the copy, the better your search results will be.

JUST THE FACTS, MA'AM

The important factor in providing content for a website is to avoid overkill. Many websites say in 1,000 words a message that could be delivered in 10. At times, it's almost as if the company has agreed to let budding artists and writers take over the development of the website to show off their skills. The best rule to remember is that your site has the potential to transmit your company's image to over 100 million people worldwide. Do you really want a frustrated writer or artist trying their hand at development?

Another problem with content is that often web houses or developers compare a website to an online brochure in their sales pitch. Many clients then unwittingly put up their brochure and receive no feedback or low hit rates and assume that the Internet is overrated. The Internet is not a place for online brochures, flyers, leaflets, etc. The web is a whole new medium and as such needs to have specific content generated for it. A company doesn't create a print ad and then run it on radio/TV or vice versa. They have separate and distinct ads used to put their message across in those different mediums. And this is what must be done for an Internet site.

A proper website is designed so that a reader can interact with it immediately. No other medium allows this. You can't walk up to a billboard and ask it questions. Nor can you get more relevant information quickly and easily from a radio/TV ad. Nor can a print ad offer you links to places to find additional information on a specific topic. However, the Internet does all this. And because it does, you must create content that encourages people to ask questions and look for more information while you have them at your site.

Studies have shown that the average reader spends approximately seven minutes in a particular website. In this time, high quality information must be made available to them in order to persuade them to remain longer in your site. And, once again, the best way to bring them in and keep them is by offering high quality content.

WEB PAGES AND WEBSITES

There is some confusion as to the difference between a web page and a website. Simple: a page is only one section of a site.

So how big can a page be? The term web "page" is really a misnomer. It's not like an A4 page, with fixed size dimensions. You can make your website as wide as you like. However, the reader will have to scroll across if the page is too big for their screen. You can also make the page as long as you want, but again, the reader will have to scroll to get information. While very few sites need horizontal scrolling, unless there was a design flaw, many use vertical scrolling.

So what exactly makes up a website? A website is a collection of web pages linked together. The only size limitation on a site is how many megabytes it takes up. Most websites are between two and five megabytes. Please bear in mind that the more programming and functionality you add to your website, the more megabytes you will require to host the site.

The most common elements found on each individual page are as follows:

Graphics, Images and Text

Together these are used to create a message and encourage a user to respond to your site. These are the "seen" elements of a page. Using the correct, appropriate graphics, text and images is required to create a successful website. See below for guidelines on how to make best use of these elements.

Page Headlines

These are the headlines running across the top of the page. These too are important for search engine registration. Keep in mind that headlines should include keywords you think people will type into the search engine in order to find your site.

Page Titles

These are hidden within the HTML code. However, they're required for successful search engine registration. When creating your pages in HTML, the title command <TITLE> should be followed by the name you want to call the page; for example, <TITLE>Contact Information</TITLE>.

Meta Tags

These too are imbedded into the HTML code and don't physically appear on the site for the reader to see. Meta tags are simple key descriptive words used to describe your site and company service. Search engines will read these tags and base their results on them.

E-mail Links

Are similar to hypertext links except they link you to an e-mail address and open an e-mail message box, enabling the reader to send an e-mail to a generic (info@domain.com) or specific (jhutch@domain.com) address.

The most common pages and features found in a website are:

Interactive Form

This can either be a contact form or order form of some description. When developing your form, you'll require not only HTML but also a language known as Perl (Practical Extraction and Report Language) in order to develop a CGI (Common Gateway Interface) script. The CGI script is what enables your browser to interact with a programme located on a web server. Perl is used as a CGI script because it can break down the information on the form and present it in a readable format. Without using

Perl, it could be difficult to understand the data required either to answer a visitor's question or to complete an order.

Site Map

Usually a page that shows how the site is split into various sections. If constructed properly, each page or section should have a hypertext link to transfer you directly to the specific section you require.

FAQs

This is short for Frequently Asked Questions. In this section of a site, you should find answers to common questions. This is to allow the reader to find answers to their questions without having to read through your entire site or contact you by e-mail to ask you the question and wait for you to answer it.

Search Facility

This is a programme used to comb the site looking for specific information. Once again, this is usually a Perl programme; however, it can also be written in C or C++, depending on the programmer. Perl is recommended, as it can run on all three platforms: Windows, Mac and Unix.

Shopping Basket

Many e-commerce sites have recently added a shopping basket facility. This allows the reader to order products, total the cost of products ordered, add applicable taxes, add shipping and handling costs, choose a method of payment (cheque or credit card) and create an invoice, all at the same time. This saves the reader from having to fill out an order form several times for several different products.

HTML EDITORS: WHAT THEY ARE AND WHICH ONE IS RIGHT FOR YOU

Before buying or even using a HTML editor, the first thing you should do is learn the basics of HTML. There are numerous training companies, books and information on the Internet about HTML and how to use it. It is essential that you know how and why the editor is working. For example, when creating tables, it's very hard to get them exactly as you want. If you create them using an editor without understanding how it works, you won't be able to fine-tune them.

The next thing to find out is what type of editor will suit you best. There are two choices available to you: a WYSIWYG (What You See Is What You Get) editor; or a standard HTML editor. The best example of a WYSIWYG editor is Microsoft's FrontPage. Netscape uses a poor man's version called Composer. The advantage of this type of editor is that whatever you design on your computer screen is close to what will appear live on the Internet. The editor creates the required HTML code behind the scenes. You don't need to have a great understanding of HTML. They are especially good at creating tables.

One of the biggest disadvantages of WYSIWYG editors is that they create far too much unnecessary code, making your site far bigger than it needs to be.

A standard HTML editor displays the original HTML code. Its advantage lies in the fact that it will create a command, such as inserting an image, by the click of a mouse button, making it unnecessary to type in the raw HTML code for inserting an image. However, its disadvantage is that you must have a good understanding of HTML to know exactly what you're doing.

There are numerous freeware and shareware HTML editors available. To get one, go to http://www.tucows.com and follow the download instructions. Tucows divides its HTML editors into beginners and advanced; choose whichever one suits you best. There are very few free WYSIWYG editors.

Let's examine some of the more popular HTML editors.

Microsoft FrontPage

As mentioned above, this is one of the more popular editors. As a WYSIWYG editor, its interface is much like any other Microsoft product. You can add images, text and graphics by clicking on the spot where you want the item to appear and inserting the image or simply start typing. Text can be manipulated in much the same way as in Microsoft Word. The biggest advantage FrontPage has over raw coding or a non-WYSIWYG editor is its ability to handle tables. As noted previously, tables are difficult to get 100 per cent correct using raw code.

FrontPage also helps create frames and comes complete with pre-constructed page templates (layouts). This makes it easy to choose a design for your site. Another big plus is that it comes complete with an image programme called Image Composer, which works much like Photoshop.

However, FrontPage has a few limitations. For example, because most people use the templates when creating their site in FrontPage, they all have a similar look and feel. One FrontPage site looks much like any other FrontPage site, unless you learn how to use the programme without using the templates, which requires knowledge of HTML. The other major disadvantage, as stated, is the amount of code FrontPage generates. Someone with a good working knowledge of HTML should be able to create a website with half the amount of HTML coding that FrontPage uses to create a site. Also, be prepared for FrontPage to use a lot of memory space. Your computer should have at least 16 MB of RAM (32 or 64 would be better) and at least 20 MB of hard disk space (50 is not out of the question).

Standard HTML Editors

Most non-WYSIWYG editors are similar in that they input coding commands on your page without you needing to type in the entire code for creating that specific function. To start with, when coding raw HTML, you need a programme such as Notepad (PC) or Simple Text (Mac). This allows the file to be saved as a .htm or html file easily. To add images or highlight text such as bold or italics, you would normally have to create the raw code by hand. However, with a HTML editor, these simple commands, and even more complex ones such as adding tables, can be created by the simple click of a mouse.

Here is an example of a basic HTML coded page. To code this page without using an editor, you would have to type all the commands in yourself.

```
<HTML>
<HEAD>
<TITLE>My First Page</TITLE>
</HEAD>
<BODY BGCOLOR="WHITE">
<p>
<FONT="ARIAL, HELVETICA SIZE=2 COLOR = Black>
This is my first page created in HTML
<p>
<IMG SRC=pic1.gif"width=125 height=125 border=0>
<p><b>By Jim Hutchinson</b>
</BODY>
</HTML>
```

While this is a very basic page — simply stating that this is my first HTML page, my name and a picture — and seems easy to complete, remember that the more complex and design-heavy you require a page to be, the more you must use HTML.

The advantage that this editor has is that by clicking the "new page" button, the initial HTML tag is created along with a page title and head tags. You can add an image by clicking the "add image" icon; or bold, italicise or underline text by clicking on the required icon.

The best advice before buying or even trying a HTML editor is to learn more about HTML and its functions. The latest version of HTML at the time of writing is 4.0. However, even if a site uses an older version, there shouldn't be any problems, even with the latest browsers.

GRAPHICS, IMAGES AND TEXT — HOW TO USE THEM PROPERLY

Now that we understand the need for high quality content, let's look at how to develop it properly. Text, images and graphics should load quickly and be cleanly designed. People don't want to wait for the graphics and information to load. They want it to appear almost instantaneously. Designers and web developers know this is next to impossible, but if you use clean design and compress the images, they can load quickly enough.

Text should be written in bullet points with a hypertext link to more complete information. For example, if you go to a car site looking for information on how restore a gas tank, it is highly unlikely you will want to read reams of information on the famous people who own a 1998 blue Mercedes. If the site uses content rules properly, you should be able to find a link to car maintenance and then another link to the gas tank restoration process (see Figures 2.1 and 2.2).

Figure 2.1: The Car Care Website . . .

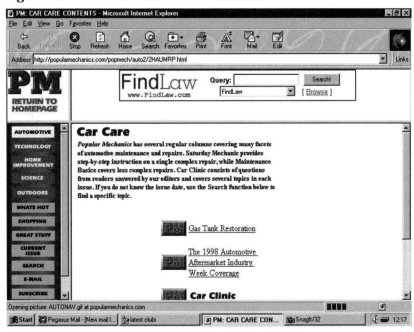

Figure 2.2: . . . and the Restoration Process Page

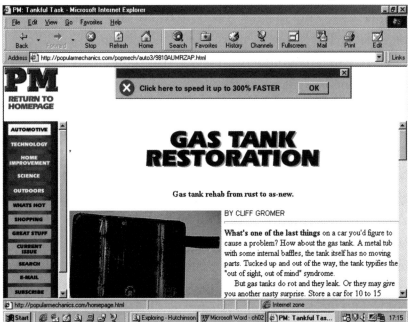

As far as text is concerned, be extremely careful about spelling, punctuation and grammar. Nothing says to potential customers that your company is careless and lacks detailed focus more than numerous mistakes in the copy. You probably spend a great deal of time making sure a brochure is correct; do the same for your website.

When adding images and graphics to a site, they must relate to the copy. Just because an image looks good doesn't necessarily mean you should use it. The simple rule is: if it's not appropriate, drop it.

Images must back up what the text is saying and help explain the idea to the reader. Let's look at the car site again. We see a picture of a 1955 Corvette restored to its original condition. If this picture is placed alongside steps on how to replace a cracked block (part of the engine), it doesn't really support the text message. However, if you put images of the cracked block at various stages of repair, the images and the text now match. Pick your images wisely and use only as many as are necessary. Try to use no more than five per page.

Also, when dealing with images, use thumbnails (small versions of the image) where possible, and include hypertext links to a larger version of the same image with additional detailed information. For example, Heritage Crystal sell their products via the Internet. If you look at their site, on one page you will find small pictures of the various products (Figure 2.3). By clicking on the image, you are taken to a larger image of the same product (Figure 2.4). This shows more detail and additional information about this specific product. The advantage of this is simple: if you want more detailed information concerning a specific product, you can easily obtain it. If you don't, you aren't required to download information that is useless to you.

Figure 2.3: Heritage Crystal's Product Page

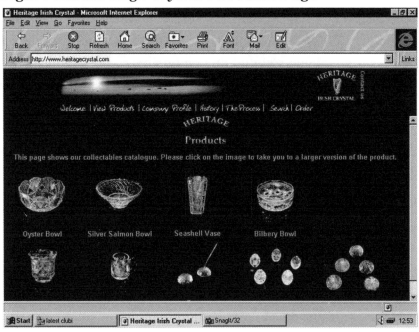

Figure 2.4: Clicking on a Thumbnail for More Detail

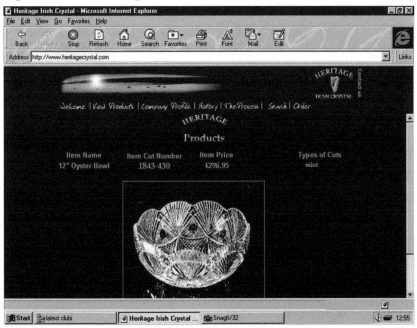

The reason why content must load quickly, be easy to find and summarise all information is simple: people tend to equate time spent online with money. After all, it is costing the price of a local telephone call and during business hours the cost can mount up. Therefore, by giving your reader access to accurate and useful information, delivered as quickly as possible, they can choose what they want and spend less time online.

Also, people's attention can only be held for so long. After a while, their minds lose focus and start to wander, they get bored and leave your site. If users feel too much information is presented, or they aren't getting a clear answer to their questions, they leave and may never come back. What's the point? They got nothing from the site during the last visit. The best advice on content is the KISS principle — Keep It Simple, Stupid.

CONTENT FAQS

Q. What do you mean by content?

A. Content can be many things. It really includes all text, images, graphics, and computer programs used in creating your site.

Q. Why should content change on a regular basis?

A. In order to encourage someone to buy your product or service, or even to contact you, they must typically visit your site at least three times. The only way to keep them coming back is to provide informative, high quality content that changes frequently.

Q. What are the things to keep in mind when developing content?

A. Make sure images load quickly, relate to the text and are simply designed. You should have no more than five images per page. Ensure that text is written in journalistic style (inverted pyramid — the most important facts first). If people require more information on the topic, they can click on a hypertext link and be taken to the additional material.

Q. How much text should go on each page?

A. As little as is needed to explain your idea or concept to the reader. Do not overkill on an idea.

Q. Do I have to produce content myself or are there companies who can do this for me?

A. No, you don't have to produce content yourself. You can hire a freelance writer or designer to produce content for you. However, before hiring such a person, make sure they are experienced in developing content for the web. There are also a number of companies who create generic content on a specific product or service for websites. For example, a widget manufacturer could buy generic information on widgets for use in part of their website. However, you should be prepared to include self-generated content specific to your own company in the site as well.

Q. What is the difference between self-generated content and generic content and which is best?

A. Self-generated content is material that is created by you (or someone you hire). It is specific to your organisation and reflects your values and message. Generic content, on the other hand, is content that, while specific to an industry, is very general in its language or design. As to which is best — it all depends on what you are doing. A good website can incorporate both without much trouble. Let's look at our widget website again. You could use self-generated content for information specific to our product and services, while generic content could cover what a widget is, what it does and its history. Let's face it, a widget is a widget is a widget, but your self-generated content would explain why your widgets are better.

Q. I have heard that free graphics are available online; is this true?

A. Yes, free graphics are available online. However, before rushing off to get some, you should remember the old adage: "You get what you pay for." Most free graphics are similar to Clip Art in that they are very generic and most look tacky. They look exactly like what they are — free images. Using free graphics is often the sign of an organisation that lacks professionalism. I would recommend getting a designer to create original graphics, whether they be a graphic arts student, a professional from a design company or one of your own employees. As long as they have experience with a design package and you are confident of their abilities, they should be able to create your site graphics for you.

3

SEARCH ENGINES — THE NECESSARY EVIL

Search engines are not the miracle cure!

Search engines will not on their own make your site successful. They are only one step in the marketing and promotion process. Rankings themselves will not create a run of traffic to your site or be the deciding success factor; many other marketing and promotional activities will need to be used. Search engines are, however, an important step in the overall marketing of the site.

So why should you worry about search engines? Although they will not guarantee higher readership figures, they are a great way to attract first-time visitors to your site. For example, if a user is looking for, say, information on widget manufacturing, instead of guessing where a site is located they'll go to a search engine, type in "widget" and see what results are returned. This is the primary reason to register with search engines. And because there are numerous engines used by various companies and groups of people, you must register with both the major and industry-specific ones in order to create the best chance of being found.

Registering with a search engine is only half the job. Like a website, the hard work begins once the initial task is completed. You must check and verify listings and results based on keywords frequently (at least quarterly). There's no point in being in the search engine if you are the 157th entry (at least seven pages into the results). No one will find you. Keeping your site in the top 50 entries is hard, time-consuming work, but it must be done to make your website a success.

STRATEGIC KEYWORDS AND PHRASES

In order to attract users to the site, you will have to develop a list of strategic keywords and phrases for use by the search engines. These are words and phrases you think people will type into the engine in order to find you. For example, a fly fishing site would use the words "fly", "fishing", "catch", "bait", "hook", or whatever potential search engine users might type (see Figures 3.1 and 3.2) These keywords should be used in your page title, your page headlines, and at the top of text pages.

Figure 3.1: Searching for Websites on Fly Fishing . . .

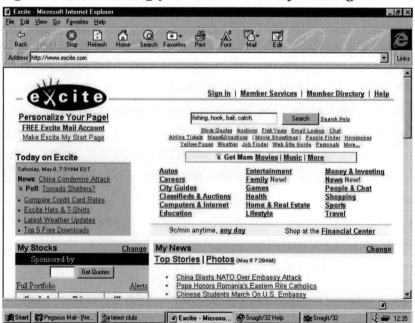

Figure 3.2: . . . Produces the Following Results

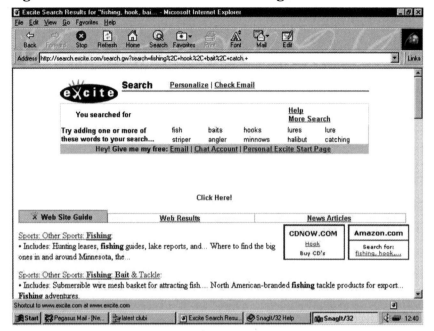

Remember when creating unique keywords to make them somewhat different. There is no point in going to all the trouble of creating these words if everybody else is using them. If your company manufactures PCs, there's no point in using the word "computer". In that case, users will find thousands of sites and yours may not be at the top of the list. If you are unsure of the keywords to use, ask someone who knows the industry or who can take a fresh look at your organisation to describe your business and the appropriate words to use.

One of the most important rules, which far too many web houses and developers forget to follow, is to use ALT tags for your graphic images. Search engines can't read images, but by using an ALT tag, part of the HTML language, you can use keywords to describe the image. These descriptive keywords will enable your listing to achieve a higher placing in the results page. The following is an example of some ALT tags used on the Angel website (see Case Study in Chapter 8). The alt tag command is used in the img src command line.

```
<img src="img/angels2.gif" width=192 height=194 align=right valign=top>
alt="[Watch the Moving Angel]"
</td></tr>
</table>
```

SUBMITTING YOUR SITE TO A SEARCH ENGINE

Now let's look at how to submit your site to a search engine. You have a choice: you can follow the old-fashioned manual approach or you can use one of the newer submission services. Submission services and programs are designed to allow the user to fill out one or two forms and then register with 20 or more search engines, depending on the service or program.

Unfortunately, in my view the choice depends on whether you want a successful website or not. If you do, then you must register the old-fashioned way, by hand. In other words, you will have to register your site by going to each search engine and registering your URL separately. However, if all you want is to be in these search engines, by all means use the submission tools.

What's the difference between the manual way and the submission programmes? Very simple: all engines have their own rules and guidelines for submission. Lycos is different from Excite, which is different from Infoseek, and so on, and while the submission services can contact the engines and submit your information, they may not be aware of all the necessary requirements for high engine placement. Also, they will not monitor and re-register you URL if necessary. The best rule of thumb for search engine registration is that you get what you pay for. If you pay $49 to be registered with 1,000 search engines — and yes, there are services that will do this — then don't expect a great return on your investment.

MONITORING YOUR LISTINGS

Once you have registered with the major search engines, you should monitor your listings frequently and verify that your URL is still in the database — occasionally you will be removed. You also should keep an eye out to make sure you are in the top 50 listings. As noted earlier, people seldom go beyond the third or fourth page of the results and if you are not there you won't be seen. It takes a lot of work and monitoring to keep your site in the top 50. You will have to resubmit your URL and redevelop meta tags if you fall out of the top 50 — and keep in mind that submission services do not do this.

You should develop and maintain a linking strategy with related but non-competitive sites. For example, if you make widgets, you may want to link to a widget accessories manufacturer. Why? There are two reasons. As mentioned above, search engines are not the only way people find your site. As a matter of fact, many people will come in by clicking on a link in another site. Secondly, some engines such as MetaCrawler will give a higher ranking to a site with a large number of links running off it. See Chapter 4 for further detail on developing a cross-linking strategy.

Another task that should be performed regularly is to examine the competing pages with the highest rankings using your keywords. This allows you not only to see what your competition is doing, but also to see what keywords people are or are not using. After all, you need to stay in the top 50 and you need to know who is above you, or below you, and why. Let's admit it: not having your URL in the first three pages of the results section on a major search engine is like having your advertisement in the middle of the ocean — it may look pretty, but very few people will see it.

SEARCH ENGINES — HOW THEY WORK

Now it's time to get just a bit more complicated and technical. Many people are confused about what a search engine is, what it is not, what it does, how it does it and why. In this section we'll look at these questions.

A search engine is an Internet product with three distinct components: a spider or crawler; a catalogue or index; and a computer program. These components work together seamlessly to find keywords for a user. How does it do this? The spider constantly searches the web looking for sites. When one is found, it checks the index or catalogue to see if the site has already been added. If you are not in the index, you will be added. If you are in the index, it will check to see if your listing has changed and update the entry as required. Finally, when a user types in a keyword, the program runs through the index finding the keywords and then returns the results to the user. The only time a person is involved in the search process is when they write the computer program or make updates, etc. However, there are differences in how these parts are created and how they run. This is why different search engines produce different results. Search programmes within a particular website work in a similar way.

Now to really confuse you: let's look at directories. Directories are not search engines. Although they may have the look and feel of engines, they don't use the three distinct components of search engines. They have an index and they're searchable, but they don't spider the web. Instead, they rely on human editors to add sites to the catalogue. So what are the best known directories? One of the world's most popular sites, Yahoo, is actually a directory and not a search engine.

Let's confuse you even more and discuss hybrid search engines. These are a cross between a directory and a search engine. They contain the three required components and functionality of search engines plus one added ingredient that doesn't appear in normal search engines — a human editor. The editor, as in a directory, reviews and decides which sites should appear in the catalogue.

Search engines clearly do an amazing job. They can search millions of entries in a database and find your keyword matches very quickly. Not bad for something that doesn't have the ability to ask questions, pass judgement or rely on past experience to find what it's looking for, like you or I could.

Now we know how search engines find websites using their three component parts. But how do they rank the results of our search? Let's look at the two principles of search engine operation: location and frequency. If you go into a shop, you are more likely to buy something if it's prominently displayed near the front of the shop. Similarly, the location of keywords for the search engine will mean the difference between succeeding or failing in your registration exercise. When they're looking for keywords, engines will look at pages and the closer to the top the keywords appear, the better the placement in the results page.

Frequency is the second principle. The more times a keyword appears on your page, the better the results will be. Therefore, when developing content, keep in mind potential keywords that people may use to search for your site and add them to your copy — though be sure you don't add them out of context just so they'll be there.

Now you know why your site is ranked 157th! To improve your ranking, use the principles of location and frequency by including what you believe are important keywords in page titles and top body copy. Keep in mind not to repeat keywords for the purpose of tricking the engine. This is called *spamming* and most search engines have ways of catching cheaters. Punishment for spamming can range from being placed at the bottom of the results page to outright removal from the index.

Finally, one last reason why placement on the engines varies: technology. While each search engine uses the three main components, they all developed differently and as such work differently from each other. Some engines spider the web more frequently and add more sites to their index, while others are designed to hold more information. For example, one of the largest search engines is Alta Vista, which indexes only one-third of all websites. It would be much simpler if all search engines worked the same, but unfortunately they don't.

SEARCH ENGINES — WHICH SITES TO REGISTER WITH

Many people ask which search engines they should be registered with. The answer is simple: the ones that are important to your site. These are the engines that are frequently used and searched and also industry-specific engines and directories.

The advantages of using a major search engine are twofold: your site will be listed in a recognised engine used by people who want dependable results; and the technology driving the engine will be kept up-to-date and be well serviced.

Also, many experts have cited the 80/20 rule. This means that 80 per cent of web users use only 20 per cent of the available search engines — though, in my opinion, the ratio is more like 95/5.

Below are a list of UK, Irish-specific and general search engines and directories you should register with. Where an address has an alternative ".com" or ".co.uk" ending, the former will be returned if you are searching the web generally, while the latter will be shown by searches of UK sites only.

UK and Irish Search Engines and Directories

*   Mirago — http://www.mirago.co.uk. This is a UK directory giving the reader not only UK-based sites, but also weather information, city and regional maps and a wealth of other information.

*   Nice One — http://www.niceone.com. This is a hybrid directory. You can search a site or pick a topic to search under. When registering with Nice One, remember that they take about 2–4 weeks to add your site to the database.

*   Search Ireland — http://www.searchireland.com. This is one of the newest Irish search engines. It breaks down by topic or you can make a specific keyword search. You can also subscribe to their newsletter, keeping you up-to-date on the latest happenings and changes at the engine.

*   Swift Kerna Ireland — http://swift.kerna.com. Looks and feels much like Yahoo. It lists both Irish and Irish-interest sites. Your site is usually added within 1–2 weeks from posting.

*   AltaVista — http://www.altavista.com (or .co.uk). Recently acquired by Compaq, Alta Vista is one of the largest search engine on the web in terms of pages indexed, and is a particular favourite among researchers. Alta Vista recently paid the highest amount for its domain name — $3.35 million — after negotiating a deal with the registered owner.

- Excite — http://www.excite.com (or .co.uk). One of the most popular Internet search engines. Its database of sites is used to power AOL Netfind and Netscape. This is the only search engine not to use meta tags to help rank results (see below). Sites are rated on the frequency and location of keywords in page titles and body copy. If you can only register with one search engine, this is the one I would recommend. A recent *USA Today* poll pegged Excite as the most popular search engine, even better than Yahoo.

- HotBot — http://www.hotbot.com. Wired Digital's entry into the search engine market. The site is powered by the Inktomi search engine and is another of the largest databases of sites. Takes 6–8 weeks to be placed in the database.

- Inktomi — http://www.inktomi.com. Inktomi also powers several other engines. While they all tap into the same index, results may vary because Inktomi allows other engines to use a common index yet make themselves look different.

- Infoseek — http://www.infoseek.com (or .co.uk). Currently indexes approximately 30 million URLs. Infoseek also runs a directory separate from its search engine. Sites are listed by topic, and editors pick which sites appear.

- LookSmart — http://www.looksmart.com. This is a directory, not a search engine, and as such is the closest rival to Yahoo. It currently lists about 300,000 web sites.

- Lycos — http://www.lycos.com (or .co.uk). One of the oldest search engines on the Internet and one of the most popular. However, it is one of the smaller independent engines around today.

- Yahoo — http://www.yahoo.com (or .co.uk). Lists approximately 1 million web sites. The thing you must remember about Yahoo is that it's a directory — not a search engine — and as such doesn't catalogue all Internet sites. Yahoo will make a search engine available to users if no links to requested information can be found.

Note: It takes approximately anywhere from 4–8 weeks to be found in the databases of the major search engines.

META TAGS

What are these wonderful things that we hear so much about and how is our site doomed to failure if we don't use them? Firstly, meta tags, while important, will not determine the success or failure of your site; they merely help push you higher in search engine listings. Secondly, meta tags are not the magic cure for search engine ills.

Meta tags provide keywords and descriptions on pages that lack required text. A frames page, for example, needs meta tags. When constructing a site using frames, two separate pages are joined together to create a third. For example, a top frame that remains constant throughout the site is combined with a "main" frame to create the home page everyone sees when they first enter the site. Meta tags must be placed on the top and main pages in order to allow the search engine to read the tags on the home page.

Meta tags might also boost your page's relevancy. However, simply including a meta tag doesn't guarantee that your site will jump to the top of the results page.

There are several meta tags, but the most important for search engine indexing are the description and keywords tags. The description tag returns a description of the page in place of the summary the search engine would ordinarily create. The

keywords tag provides keywords for the search engine to asso-
ciate with your page.

Let's take a look at how meta tags can improve the search
engine results. For example, if your site were called "Welcome
to Ireland" it might have a large graphic of a leprechaun
dancing around a shamrock (a really bad front page, by the
way). However, down near the bottom of the page we have information on Irish history, geography, politics, etc. Because of
your text placement, the site wouldn't show up very high in
search results.

To fix this problem, we could add meta tags and page titles
to the site, making it look like this:

<HEAD>
<TITLE>Ireland: The Country</TITLE>
<META name="description" content="Everything you wanted
to know about Ireland from its people to its history">
<META name="keywords" content="Ireland, Irish, history, ge-
ography, people, stories">
</HEAD>

Now your listing will look something like this in search engines
that support the descriptions tag:

Ireland: The Country
Everything you wanted to know about Ireland from its people to
its history

Notice how the description matches what's in the description
tag. That's exactly what the meta description tag does. It lets
you control the description that appears in the search engine.

What about the meta keywords tag? It gives your page a
chance to come up if someone types in any combination of the
words listed. For example, someone might enter *Ireland his-*

tory, which will match with one of the keywords in the tag. Without that tag, there would be no chance at all, since "Ireland history" doesn't appear on the page or in the description tag.

Should you have different variations for keywords, such as shown in the example? This may help you with some search engines and not at all with others.

Remember, you are using these tags to help make up for the lack of text on your pages, not as a way to successfully anticipate every keyword variation a person might enter into a search engine. The only hope you have of ever doing that is to have good, descriptive pages with good titles and text that is not buried on the bottom of the page by JavaScript, frames tags or tables. The meta tags are a tool to get around these problems.

SEARCH ENGINE REGISTRATION TIPS

Now that we know what search engines are and how they work, let's get down to the real exercise of registering with them. Here is a list of dos and don'ts when registering with search engines:

Some Dos:

- Watch spelling of keywords.
- Add common variations of spellings or misspellings for different words (for example, color, colour, interest, intrest). Not everyone surfing the web has English as a first language and they may misspell many common words.
- Use meta tags and descriptive keywords.
- Monitor your search engine placement on a regular basis.

- Re-register if you fall out of the top 50.

- Add and change keywords and meta tags frequently (especially if you fall from the top 50).

- Frequently repeat keywords at the beginning of the editorial copy in your site.

Some Don'ts:

- Don't put hidden text on your website, such as same coloured text as the background. In other words, don't use white text on a white background so that the keywords are invisible to visitors, but are read by the search engine.

- Don't use keywords that are not related to your website. For example, if you are selling cars, don't use sex, women, etc. Yes, you'll get visitors, but they'll quickly leave after seeing that your site is not what they were looking for.

- Don't use computer programs (e.g. Perl or Java Scripts) to re-direct visitors to a different version of your site than that which they would normally see.

- Don't make different versions of the same page in hopes that one of them will rank higher in search results.

The dos and don'ts of search engine registration are important so that you can gain a top entry and keep it there. High placement in a search engine results page is important for three reasons:

1. People who are looking for information on a specific topic come to the search engines first. When they find the results, they usually only read the top 50 entries.

2. Once a person finds an engine they like, they stick with it. They very seldom change from a search engine they like.

3. Most readers won't go beyond the third page of listings, which means if you appear as the 150th entry (approximately the seventh or eighth page), your entry won't be seen and nobody will come to your site.

The most frequent question I'm asked concerning search engine placement is: "My competitor is at the top of the list — how did they do that?" To put it bluntly, they did it in one of three ways:

- *They got lucky*: a lot of websites do get lucky and appear at the top of the engine. These sites are easy to beat by using meta tags and high placement of keywords in the copy and page titles.

- *They cheated*: Alta Vista rejects over 60 per cent of the daily submissions they receive because of cheating practices known as spamming. As discussed earlier, engines have the technology to catch you, or your competitors quickly complain about the cheating, and penalties for cheating range from lower placement in the results to being removed from the search engine altogether.

- *They planned*: Site managers learned how the engines work and how to prepare pages that are easily found and ranked highly by the engines.

SEARCH ENGINE FAQS

Q. What is a search engine?

A. A search engine is a computer program used to catalogue the Internet, create a database of available sites and then allow it to be searched by users.

Q. What is a directory and how is it different from a search engine?

A. A directory is similar to a search engine in that a searchable database is created allowing users to search for information. However, the primary difference between a search engine and a directory is the human factor. To obtain a listing in a directory, you must submit your URL (web address) to an editor. This person decides if you are going to be listed with the directory. The best example of a directory is Yahoo. Search engines don't involve human input outside of the programming.

Q. What is the underlying technology of search engines?

A. A search engine is made up of three distinct parts which it uses to work. The *spider* crawls the Internet looking for a website. It then indexes sites and pages in a *database*. When you go to search the site it will then use its *program* to find the keywords and return the search results.

Q. How come my site can't be found high up in the results pages?

A. The main reason is that you most likely haven't followed the location and frequency rules. Engines work on one basic principle: repetition of keywords high up in the copy. When the program looks for keywords in your site, it checks page titles, descriptions and body copy for the keywords. The more often and higher up on the page they appear, the better return results you'll get.

Q. Are search engine submission services all they claim to be?

A. The answer is yes, but with a qualification. Like most businesses they do what they say they will do — submit your site to numerous search engines and directories for an agreed price, usually about US$50. However, this will not create a successful search engine registration policy. While most will do what they claim, they don't do the little things required to get high placement in an engine. For example, they don't monitor and re-register your site when required; they don't create meta tags for your site. Placement results in each of the search engines are your responsibility. It's better to be placed high in the top 10 search engines, than to appear in 500 different ones five pages into each results section.

Q. How come I get different results in different search engines?

Each engine is programmed slightly differently. While they all work on the same basic principles of location and frequency, they report their results different. Also, some search engines such as Excite do not use meta tags. Others spider the web at a different rate and therefore add site URLs at difference frequencies. Updates to databases may not be as frequent as with other search engines.

Q. How come it takes so long to get my URL into a search engine?

A. The average wait from the time you register with a search engine to the time you are listed is 6–8 weeks. The reason is simple: with so many new sites coming online, there is a back-log in adding new sites to the engine's database.

Q. What is meant by spamming a search engine?

A. Spamming a search engine is basically cheating. This is done in a few ways. Firstly, you put keywords on all pages in the same colour as the background of your pages. For example, if your site is black text on a white background, you then type a list of keywords in white type. This makes the keywords invisible to the reader, but not the search engine. According to rules of frequency and location, you should earn a higher placement in the results. Don't count on this! Engines have the technology to catch you and remove your site from its catalogue.

Secondly, you could create numerous versions of your home page with different keywords and find out which one works best in different search engines. However, the engine constantly updates its listings and if it finds too many versions of your home page, it will remove yours because it believes you're spamming them.

Remember that the penalty for spamming an engine can range from being placed at the bottom of the results to being removed altogether from the engine.

4

PUBLICITY: WHY YOU NEED IT

Your site is up and running. Content has been verified and you have registered with both Irish and international search engines. Now it's time to sit back and count the hits, right? Not quite yet! The job of marketing and promoting the site must now be completed. After all, if you don't announce your site to the world, no one will even know it exists. Search engine registration may be a requirement for having a successful website, but it is only one. You must market and promote the site on a regular basis if it's to be successful. Remember: not all of the people surfing the web will find your site using a search engine. To manage a successful website, it must be marketed using the following methods:

- Developing a cross-linking strategy

- Giving out additional, unrequested information

- Answering all e-mails within 24 hours

- News group announcements

- Discussion groups

- What's New announcement lists

- Mailing lists

- Developing an Internet newsletter

- Developing surveys and questionnaires on site

- Buying your own domain name

- Putting your URL address on company stationery

- Obtaining press coverage.

So how is marketing on the Internet any different from marketing in one of the traditional media? To be honest, this is still such a new area that no one is sure. The only thing we know is that traditional methods don't work on the web, mainly because of the interactive nature of the Internet, which is not available in other media.

Nothing like the Internet has come before and we're still feeling our way around. Think back to the first days of television and how the early commercials were developed. The announcer sat there talking to the audience, just like on radio. It was a few years before story lines and ideas were developed and used in commercials. Today, there is a similar problem when developing, planning and creating a marketing/ promotional or advertising campaign on the Internet. People don't always use the technology properly or even understand how to drive traffic to a site. However, this still leaves us with the question of how to market on the web. Below are some strategies to consider.

DEVELOPING CROSS-LINKS (AFFINITY MARKETING)

One of the best ways to market your site is to develop a cross-linking strategy with related but non-competitive sites. For example, if you make computer hardware, you may e-mail a software company who, while they're related to your business, don't directly compete with you. They simply make software to run on your hardware. The e-mail should be used to agree on an exchange of hypertext links designed to take the user from your site to theirs or vice versa. This way, if one of their readers is interested in finding out more on computer hardware, and yours more specifically, they will come to your site and read about your products. Likewise, the reverse is true for their site. Many people return to a site by remembering where they found a link, not the address. Therefore, if a reader found your site through the software site, they're liable to return to that specific site to find you again.

Figure 4.1: Software Site Showing Links to other Sites

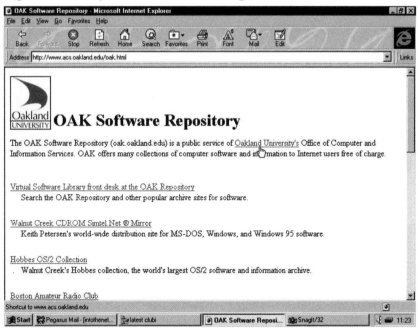

Links can be free or paid for. However, before agreeing to exchange links, even for free, examine the other website. Make sure you want to place your company name or logo on it. Verify that your company's good name and reputation will not be damaged because of the content in the other site. Remember the saying: "Your reputation precedes you." If you get involved with someone who uses unsavoury business practices, no one will trust or believe in your product or service. Also, would customers really think highly of being linked to an inappropriate site?

ADDITIONAL INFORMATION

Another way of marketing a site is to give additional, unrequested information to readers. For example, if you run a site on moving, you may give readers a checklist on how to pack properly and detailing things you should do before moving (e.g. notify the post office concerning a change of address and utility companies for turning off the electricity or telephone).

Figure 4.2: Oman's Moving Site Offers a Wealth of Useful Information

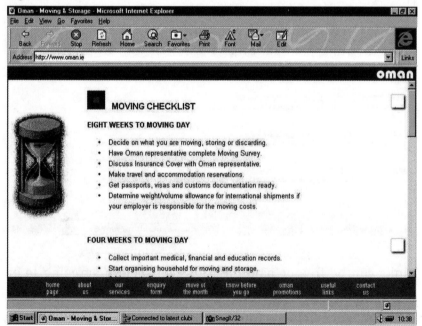

People come to the Internet for information, not sales pitches. If you want to see an ad for a moving company, you can quickly and easily pick up the Golden Pages and find information on the numerous moving companies listed. But what you can't find is the extra information to make your move easy. When using additional information, remember to follow content rules and change these tips and hints frequently.

ANSWERING ALL E-MAILS WITHIN 24 HOURS

The Internet is interactive and as such people expect immediate or very quick responses and turnaround times to questions and queries. Nothing will upset a user quicker than not receiving a response to a question, order or e-mail. All your hard work, time, effort and money will be wasted if you don't respond within 24 hours to any e-mail that comes to you. This, however, doesn't mean you have to spend all your time answering e-mails.

An auto-responder can be added to the website. Your technical department or ISP should be able to help you. This will automatically send a response to an e-mail, stating a specific message. For example, it could read:

> *"Thank you for contacting Acme Hardware Company. Your comments are important to us and we will answer your question in the next 24–48 hours."*

Remember that you must live up to whatever you promise in the auto-responder message. A responder doesn't allow you personally to answer the query. It does, however, give you time to make a well-formed and considered response.

The other rule about e-mail is to check spelling, punctuation and grammar. Too many mistakes in this area will reflect poorly on your organisation. Think of e-mail as part of your business correspondence and treat it as you would any letter to business associates.

NEWSGROUP ANNOUNCEMENTS

Newsgroups are often the forgotten part of the Internet. Most people believe the Internet and the web to be synonymous, but they are not. The web is only one part of the Internet. The Internet is made up of the World Wide Web, e-mail and newsgroups. We all know what the web and e-mail are, but not many people know and understand newsgroups.

Newsgroups are simple. They consist of a collection of like-minded people who follow or understand a specific subject area and converse using e-mail and postings on the topic. There are currently over 50,000 different newsgroups in existence, covering everything from archaeology to zoology.

Before announcing your site to the newsgroup, there are a few terms and rules you need to be aware of. The first thing you need to understand is what type of group it is. There are two basic types of newsgroups: moderated and unmoderated. A moderated newsgroup has a moderator/manager, who is appointed to run the group and usually reads all the e-mails/postings sent to the newsgroup, then posts your comments, questions, queries, etc. for the rest of the group to read. The reason a group is moderated is to keep track of what is being said, to keep the discussions focused on the topic and to make sure no inappropriate postings are made to the group.

Unmoderated newsgroups, of which there are fewer, have no moderator and therefore anyone can post anything they like at any time. Be warned: this could include libellous or offensive comments.

There are two ways to find newsgroups. You can go to a website called DejaNews (http://www.dejanews.com), and follow the instructions on how to navigate around the site and the rules they expect you to follow. Click on the new users' link for the first few visits to understand how to use the newsgroups. The second way to find various newsgroups is through your Internet Service Provider. Most will run a news server with access to the various newsgroups and information.

Before jumping off to DejaNews, there are a few rules you should understand about newsgroup postings. Do not blatantly advertise your product, service or website to group members. Most newsgroups are non-commercial enterprises and members and moderators do not take kindly to advertising. Punishment for advertising can range from being removed from the group to being "flamed" — long, nasty e-mails sent to your box, which could take you hours to get rid of.

Figure 4.3: Example of a Newsgroup

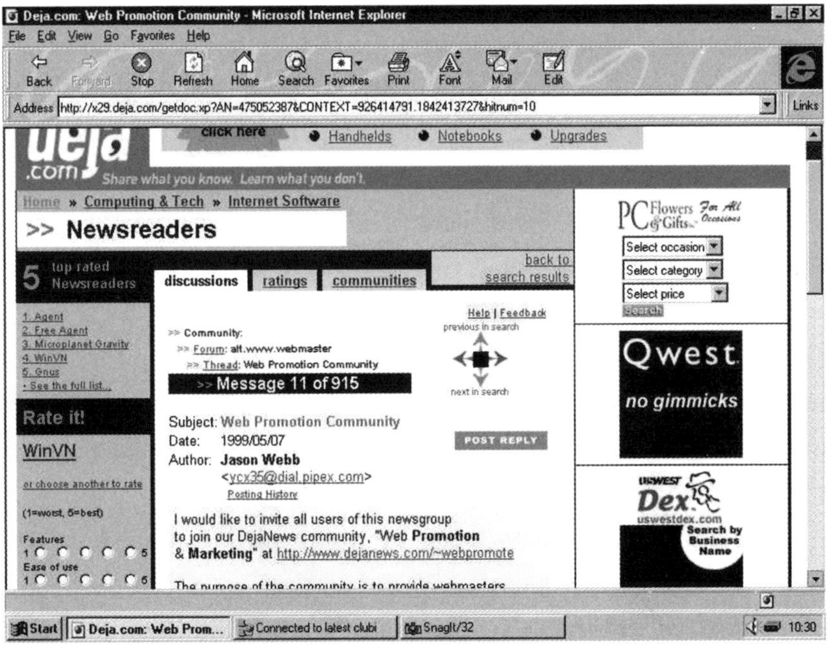

So how do you market through newsgroups? Simple: you answer questions posed by group members as an expert in that field. For example, if you own an antique shop and join the antique newsgroup, you can feel free to answer any questions posed by members of the group, stating your background to prove you are qualified in that field.

A second way is to sign all e-mail with your name, company name and website address. People can then check out your site in their own time if they want to. Your mail package should allow you to add a specialised signature to the bottom of all e-mails by using the signature option. For more information on how to set this up, check your mail package or talk with your service provider.

The next thing you should remember is not to jump into a conversation in a newsgroup — lurk for a while. As your mother always told you: "Don't interrupt!" Follow that rule for newsgroups. Just as you wouldn't walk up to two people holding a conversation and start rambling on about your latest holiday without having the slightest knowledge of what they were talking about, don't do it here.

Take a few days, read some postings, make sure you know what you want to say, how you want to say it and write and re-write it if necessary. Think of a newsgroup posting as a representative e-mail of the company. Check spelling, punctuation and grammar before sending your posting. Once you send it, stay involved in the newsgroup and try to send your postings out as much as possible.

Newsgroups can be both fun and informative. Use them well and you'll have an opportunity to market your company in a cost-effective manner. Keep in mind, however, that you must go to the newsgroup — it won't come to you.

MAILING LISTS

Similar to newsgroups, mailing lists are a collection of like-minded people coming together to discuss a certain topic. The major difference is that instead of having to subscribe to a newsgroup or going to an ISP's news server or DejaNews to look for postings, mailing list postings are sent directly to your e-mail box. You can read them every time you check your mail.

A word of warning! Get yourself a free e-mail address from one of the many sites providing them such as Yahoo, Lycos, Excite, Hot Mail, Ireland.com, etc. This way, no one on the list can obtain your personal e-mail address. There are two reasons for this. First, you may end up on someone's junk e-mail list and then be inundated with spam (junk e-mail) — everything from golf lessons to how to market your website using search engine registration. The second reason is that you don't want to subscribe to all these groups and then have to sift through hundreds of e-mails per week just to find important work-related ones.

As with newsgroups, don't advertise your product or service and remember to lurk for a few days before joining the conversation.

There are over 30,000 mailing lists in existence today. For a fairly comprehensive list of them and how to start and market your own list, visit http://www.liszt.com.

A great way of marketing your site and service to the Internet is to develop your own mailing list. Be warned, however: it takes a great deal of time, effort and energy to start, maintain and work a mailing list. The more people who join your list, the more work you will have editing e-mails and keeping conversations on track. You will also spend more time dealing with enquiries. And in the beginning you will need to spend a lot of time marketing and promoting the list.

To start your own list, you can do one of two things. You can go to http://www.onelist.com and follow their set-up guidelines. The advantage of One List is simple — it's cheaper than doing it yourself. One List provides you with both the required servers and software to operate the list. They make money by selling ad space on your postings, e-mails and messages, as well as advertising on the site.

However, if you prefer not to have advertising or think it may cheapen your list, you must do the following. Learn how to set up and pay for the list server's software and space and the technical expertise to set up and administer the hardware and software from your service provider. You will need to design and market the list, just as you do with your website, in order to make it successful. It may make more sense to find a few mailing lists and join them, but if you feel you have to start one, then check out One List and save yourself some major headaches.

DISCUSSION GROUPS

Discussion groups are very similar to newsgroups and mailing lists. The basic difference is that a newsgroup is not part of a website, but a discussion group is. A discussion group is the part of a website that allows people to interact around a chosen topic. They look and feel slightly different to a newsgroup or mailing list in that you follow threads and postings. They work by allowing the participant to read postings and then respond or put their ideas across. For an example of a discussion group, go to http://www.molson.com/bathroomwall.html.

Discussion groups can be either moderated or unmoderated, depending on how the company feels about this. Like newsgroups and mailing lists, most are moderated and all contents are checked for spelling, grammar, punctuation and libellous material. If you are the discussion list publisher, you might end up being responsible for what appears on your site.

The etiquette rules are similar to those of newsgroups, with no blatant advertising allowed. Most moderators will not allow ads to be posted.

Figure 4.4: Example of a Discussion Group

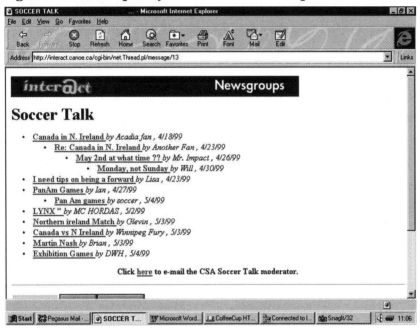

WHAT'S NEW / ANNOUNCEMENT LISTS

These are used to tell people your site has just gone live or you have a newsworthy announcement you would like to make. They are standalone sites similar to search engines. As with a search engine, you add your URL and it then becomes part of a searchable database. Unlike a search engine, these postings will be removed after a specified period. Are you really new and newsworthy six months after your site has been launched?

While these are useful for short periods of time, don't spend a lot of time and energy on them, because you're going to be removed within one to three months. However, they're worth using to announce your site, as many journalists and web reviewers look here for new and interesting websites.

DEVELOPING AN INTERNET NEWSLETTER

This too requires work and effort. You must create a newsletter specifically for the Internet. It must be written, produced and guided by Internet rules, not traditional newsletter rules. You must keep in mind that the Internet is interactive and devise ways to encourage people to respond.

Like newsgroups or mailing lists, you must monitor, update and market your Internet product. What good is a newsletter that no one reads? You must keep it topical and the information must be useful to your readers. You should update it at least monthly; weekly would be better. Newsletters are normally sent to subscribers via e-mail.

If you do decide to create an Internet newsletter, your content should follow website content rules:

- *Keep it simple*: Don't try to dazzle or baffle readers with large amounts of information and jargon. Get straight to the point and tell them exactly what you want to tell them.

- *Write in inverted pyramid style*: Like a newspaper, the most important facts go first. Then as the story progresses, you can add the details.

- *Update frequently and regularly*: If you promise to do it monthly, do it monthly. Remember this when planning your newsletter — you may suddenly run into a large amount of work and let the newsletter slide. Don't let this happen. If you promise something, you must deliver — after all, your company's reputation is at stake.

Figure 4.5: Example of an Internet Newsletter

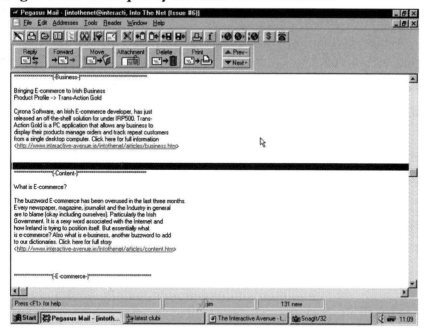

DEVELOPING SURVEYS AND QUESTIONNAIRES ON SITE

The web is the world's only truly interactive medium — use it! Nowhere else can more questions be asked and answered than on your website. This is why your website must be viewed as more than a company brochure, more than a magazine, newspaper advertisement or annual report. Because it is interactive, you need to get your readers involved with it.

Yes, you can ask them questions. Some will answer, some will not, some will be truthful, others not. Take all this into consideration if you are developing a survey to put on the website. Also, take note of the fact that not all people will respond to your questionnaire. However, it is a good way of finding out what your readers and clients think about certain ideas and concepts. You can find out what potential clients' buying habits are, their annual income, their level of education, how many kids they have, etc. Could you develop this kind of demographic information from a newspaper ad or billboard?

When developing your questions for the survey, make sure they're not loaded towards the responses you're looking for. You want answers to be honest and truthful. How else are you going to find out what is or is not working in your site?

Many sites that require a subscription form to be filled out will survey their readers and users before giving them access to a special section of the site. Some other sites will ask a "yes or no" question simply to provide interactivity. For example, a sports site might contain a feedback section with questions such as, "Was the latest team signing a good move for the team (yes or no)?" The visitor would click a checkbox or radio button for their answer. The advantage of this type of simple "yes or no" question is that it allows readers to give feedback about a topic that interests them.

A word of warning about asking people to fill out long questionnaires: many won't do it. Too many people are scared of ending up on a mailing list and being inundated with junk e-mail. Always inform the reader that any information received from the questionnaire is strictly confidential and will not be sold or given to any third party.

BUYING YOUR OWN DOMAIN NAME

Before we talk about why you should buy a domain name, let's find out what it is. According to *Wired*, a domain name is a unique set of numbers used on the Internet. Each computer on the Internet is given its own IP (Internet Protocol) address, which is in fact a series of numbers (e.g. 123.89.75.40). Since it's easier to remember a name instead of a group of numbers, the domain name was created. The name is just a substitute for these numbers. For example, the domain name for http://www.oaktreepress.com is oaktreepress.com.

Each top-level domain name has two parts: the server name (in this case oaktreepress) and a suffix, which denotes either the type of company running the site or the geographic location of the server. For example, .co.uk is for a server located in the United Kingdom, .ie is for Ireland. Other examples of domain name endings are:

- .com — used by commercial businesses, mainly US in origin

- .net — is used on a main site which would host a group of smaller sites

- .edu — is for US educational institutions

- .org — non-profit organisations

- .gov — government agencies.

A domain name is also known as a web address or URL. There are currently seven more domain endings being developed in the US because the demand for domain names is outstripping supply. Many organisations are now finding that most domain names are taken. You will only be given a domain name if it has not already been taken.

Other countries, like the UK and Ireland, use a two-letter ending for their sites. Britain uses .uk for its sites, Ireland uses .ie, Italy's is .it, France's is .fr, New Zealand's is .nz, etc. Some countries also use .co to signify a commercial site — for example, http://www.widget.co.uk. Ireland does not use the .co, as there are not enough sites to make it necessary to distinguish.

The other domain name you can use is one that is assigned by your service provider or hosting company. It looks something like this: http://www.widget.co.uk/~mycompany. If we break down this address, we see that our request goes to the domain name widget.co.uk in the UK and then to the website named "my company". It then pulls up your website and displays the information.

The problem with this type of domain name is simple. If you type http://www.widget.co.uk when looking for your company's site, you won't get it. Instead, you will be transferred to the main widget company site. You would be surprised at how many people will do this when looking for a website.

The reasons for buying your own domain name are twofold. The first one is professionalism. How would you feel about dealing with a company that only lists a postal address for its headquarters? Or an organisation that gives only a mobile contact number? The second reason is to be remembered. It is easier to type in www.widget.co.uk than something like www.widget.co.uk/~mycompany.htm.

Once you have decided to buy an address with a specific domain name, you need to choose which type to buy — .com, .co.uk or .ie. You can have any domain name you require, but the .com names are cheaper to buy and much easier and quicker to get. The cost for registering a .com name with the proper authorities (InterNic — www.internic.net) is $70 and the domain name is good for the first two years and must be renewed annually thereafter. A .co.uk name costs st£80 and is registered with Nominet (www.nominet.org.uk), which is good for two years. Finally, a .ie name costs IR£100 and is only good for one year. Also, both UCD (University College Dublin, the Irish domain name authority — www.ucd.ie) requires more paperwork to apply for a name. I would recommend only getting an Irish domain name if your company is playing up its Irish angle (for example, a company specialising in Irish family names or Irish history, etc.). Otherwise, you can obtain a .com or .co.uk suffix with less hassle and cost.

Unlike in the US, you must prove to UCD that you have rights to the name if you want a .ie suffix. In other words, if your company is named Irish Block Manufacturing, you wouldn't be entitled to the name http://www.ibm.ie, as when one thinks of IBM, Irish Block Manufacturing would probably be the last thing to come to mind. However, if you submitted http://www.ibm.com to InterNic and no one else had this name, they would simply give it to you. However, you would have to fight IBM when they came after you for taking their name. Be warned: domain names cannot be trademarked unless they're part of your existing company name. For example, Micro-soft.com can't be trademarked, but Amazon.com can be, as that is the company's name.

The last reason for buying a .com domain name is that hosting prices in the US are half of what they are in Ireland. And since it doesn't matter where you host the site, it would make sense to have a .com domain name.

PUTTING YOUR URL ADDRESS ON COMPANY STATIONERY

This is something many people forget to do. When printing new business cards, letterheads, compliment slips or any kind of company stationery, include the website address and individual e-mail addresses, if appropriate. This should be done as soon as possible.

OBTAINING PRESS COVERAGE

This is probably the most difficult promotional goal to achieve. Before developing a press release, make sure you have a news angle for the story. Just putting a site on-line is no longer an event; you must have something more before a publication will cover it. For example, you could provide information on the euro if you are a banking or financial site, or Y2K (the year 2000 problem or millennium bug) if you run a technology-related site. Keep in mind that you must have some kind of event happening before contacting the media.

Once you have a newsworthy event, there are a few rules for writing a good quality press release. First off:

- Make sure you have the editor's name and that you spell it properly. Nothing sends a press release to the wastebasket faster than having the wrong name or a spelling mistake. If you can't be bothered to pick up the phone and ask for the appropriate person and how to spell their name, why should the editor take time to read your press release?

- Make sure you are sending the press release to the right editor. It's no good sending a technology-related story to the entertainment editor. It will only end up in the bin.

Now it's time to write the press release. When creating your release, keep the following in mind:

- Write your release in inverted pyramid style. Give the most important facts first and keep them relevant. Don't go off on a tangent; stay on the topic.

- Keep the release to approximately 300 words. You need to give the editor your news, not your life story. Editors are busy people and don't have time to read more than the first few paragraphs of the release.

- Know the publication's readership. Buy a copy of the publication, view the demographics, the writing style and how they converse with their readers. Keep the tone of your press release in line with the style the publication sets for its readers.

- Try to write your release as a news story. This way, if the newspaper has a hole, which they quite often do, they might just run part of your release. To practise writing in journalistic style, try rewriting news stories, or better yet fairy tales. For example, Snow White and Seven Dwarves might read something like this: "A wedding rocked the Kingdom today as Prince Charming and Snow White were joined in holy matrimony." Keep to the facts and put the most important ones first.

After you have written your press release and found out whom to send it to, send it to them in their preferred format. If they like all releases to be e-mailed to them, then do that. However, if they prefer to have them faxed, do that instead. Always make it as easy as possible for the editor to get your release and use it.

The last point about editors is simply this: they are busy people and can be very grumpy if disturbed. Don't hassle them about your release. If they're interested, they'll contact you for more information. You'll only upset them if you phone up and ask if they've received your latest release. Most editors receive hundreds of press releases, invitations, letters, faxes, e-mails, phone calls, etc. in a week and the chances of them recalling your specific one are slim — unless you make it stand out. And if you do, they'll call looking for more information.

RELATIONSHIP MARKETING

While this may be a new term to some, the idea itself is not new. Relationship marketing, in the context of the Internet, is about taking advantage of the Internet's unique capabilities.

For example, one of the great advantages of Internet market-ing is the ability to deal one-to-many, one-to-few or even one-to-one, all at the same time.

Your site can be designed to appeal to a mass audience or to a specific target group — say, 25-year-old males who are em-ployed in middle management — or you can target your site to just one person. How can this be done? Simple — relationship marketing.

To see a great example of this type of marketing, go to www.amazon.co.uk and look around. You can browse through the site or you can pick a specific genre of books or music you like. The site will even personalise your favourite types of books or music so that they can inform you about products you are more likely to buy. If you like to read science fiction/ fantasy, for example, you probably don't need to know about the latest P.J. O'Rourke novel, but a rare and unpublished Robert Jordan book would be of interest to you.

Figure 4.6: Amazon.co.uk's Home Page

It is not only retail websites that are investing in the technology to exploit this type of marketing; so also are search engines. You can now personalise most of the major search engines to find websites that you're most likely to be interested in and avoid the ones you don't care about.

SPONSORSHIP — WHAT IT TAKES

Yes, you can gain sponsorship for your site. However, before even attempting to find a sponsor, you should use the techniques in this book to build traffic and know and understand who is coming into your site. Once you have this information, you can then look for sponsorship.

For example, if you're managing an entertainment-related site where readers can find concert listings, film, theatre, restaurant and CD reviews, interviews with artists, etc., you may decide that instead of trying to sell loads of advertising space, you may approach a beer company to see if they will sponsor the concert listings section or maybe one of the review sections.

In order to obtain sponsorship, you must have information that people will want to read and revisit on a regular basis. You must fine-tune your site and know what is working, what is not and how to change it.

PUBLICITY FAQS

Q. What is the best method to use for marketing and promoting my website?

A. There are various ways to market and promote your site. For example, you could use newsgroups or "what's new" pages, buy your own domain name, distribute press releases, develop questionnaires and surveys for your site, create an Internet newsletter, start and manage a mailing list, and so on.

Q. What is the advantage of buying my own domain name?

A. By purchasing your own address, you make it easier to find your website, your site address is easier to remember and your company appears to be more professional and to take the Internet more seriously.

Q. What's the difference between a newsgroup, discussion list and mailing list?

A. The difference between these three communications tools are in the method of delivery. A *newsgroup* is read either by opening your service provider's news server and reading the topics you are interested in or by going to http://www.dejanews.com, which is an Internet site that lists most of the available 50,000 newsgroups. A *discussion list* is created as part of your website and is only accessible by going to that specific website. A *mailing list* is created so that members do not have to surf the web at all, except to sign up for it. All questions and answers to and from the mailing list are sent directly to your e-mail box in the form of a daily digest or as each individual e-mail is sent to the moderator.

Q. Why is it important to answer e-mails promptly?

A. People expect prompt answers because they have been led to believe that the Internet, and more specifically the web, are instantaneous and therefore all questions should be answered immediately.

Q. How can I answer questions quickly, even when not at work?

A. Set-up an auto responder on your site. Your ISP should be able to help you with this. Your message should say something like: "Thank you for your e-mail. Due to a heavy volume of traffic, it may take us 24-48 hours to see to your response personally. Please bear with us and we'll get to your message. Thank you. The management of XYZ company."

Q. What is relationship marketing and how does the web exploit it?

A. Relationship marketing is a type of marketing that allows a website publisher to relate to different groups of people at the same time. You can relate on a one-to-many basis, one-to-few basis or even a one-to-one basis, all at the same time. To take advantage of relationship marketing, design your site so it welcomes return visitors and knows and understands their preferred products or services without having to tell them about all of your services.

5

MEDIA BUYING

Early to bed, early to rise . . . advertise . . .
advertise . . . advertise.

These are the immortal words of John Kroc, founder of the McDonald's fast food empire. Just because you have built the world's greatest Internet site doesn't mean anybody will beat a path to its door. You must advertise and promote the site accordingly. The previous chapter looked at general strategies for creating publicity; now it is time to enter the murky waters of Internet media planning and buying.

While media buying is part of the overall marketing and promotional process, it is just one aspect of it, just as advertising is only one part of the traditional marketing process. Many people know and understand the concept of marketing and promoting a product or service. Online advertising has created its own industry with its own terminology and expressions, which need to be understood if they are to be used effectively. This chapter should help you understand the unique ways of promoting your website using online advertising.

This chapter is not for the weak of heart. It is also not for people trying to market and promote a site on a shoestring budget. You must devote adequate resources to buying Internet space for advertising. Granted, it is cheaper than traditional advertising, but it still requires a significant budget to be successful in driving traffic to your site.

The big problem with Internet advertising is that it is still in its infancy, especially in the UK and Ireland, and could be difficult to understand and arrange on your own. For example, if you're a soap manufacturer and want to reach a large television audience, you can simply advertise during the commercial break in *Coronation Street* and reach approximately 20 million UK and Irish viewers. The question for the Internet is: How do you reach those same viewers using its technology and statistics?

Many traditional UK and Irish advertising agencies have avoided media planning and buying for the Internet like the plague, simply because charging and rating methods are confusing and ambiguous, to say the least, and they change from site to site. For example, some sites will charge monthly, some charge based on impression, some charge based on click-thrus. There is no real set standard for buying space on the Internet, which makes it confusing and difficult to do.

Also, contacting individual sites can be a long and tiresome process. First you have to find a specific site (worse than trying to find a needle in a haystack), then contact the publisher, find out the user demographics and charges, and finally negotiate a price for the advertising space. Then you have to construct a workable banner ad.

And you basically have two choices in terms of buying advertising space on the Internet: you can either do it all by yourself or hire a specialist agency to conduct this work for you.

MEDIA BUYING TERMS

In order to get to the heart of Internet media buying or selling, you'll need to understand some terms:

- *Hits*: This was how readership figures were established in the early days of the Internet. Often it was heard that a site got 2,000 hits per month. But what does this really mean? A hit occurs when someone enters a page within your site and starts to download files. Unfortunately, hits do not mean actual readers. Every file, whether it be a graphic, text or image, counts as a hit when downloaded by the user. In other words, if you have five images along with text on a page, and the user downloads your page to their computer, six hits will be registered for the site. Six-to-one also happens to be the average figure for hits to readership ratio.

- *Page View/Impression*: This is now the statistic used to replace the hit rate. This is the actual number of visitors who come into your site. One visitor represents one page view/impression. Note that most companies only recognise one page view per day from a unique IP address.

- *CPC (Cost per Clickthru)*: This is a cost measurement. Many website publishers will charge based on a cost per clickthru. This means you're charged on the amount of people who click on your banner ad, which takes them to your site.

- *CPM (Cost per Thousand)*: This is a traditional advertising measurement. You pay based on the number of people who see the banner ad. For example, the average price you pay for a banner ad should be £50–£70 CPM. What this really means is that you're paying 5 pence for every person who sees the ad.

- *Banner Ad*: A graphically designed ad, usually a GIF, measured in pixels (average size is 468 pixels wide by 60 pixels high, limited to 8 Kilobytes in memory size). Animation can also be used, as long as the program used to view the animation is small enough.

- *Click*: When a visitor clicks on a banner ad, they are automatically transported to the advertiser's web page.

- *Click Rate*: The percentage of visitors who click on a banner ad.

- *Ad Broker or Network*: This is a company that purchases advertising space from publishers and resells it to people looking to place advertising on high traffic sites. For selling space, I don't recommend you contact any ad network until your site is generating at least 100,000 impressions per month.

- *Banner exchange services*: These are services that exchange banner ads with other sites, usually on a proportional basis to the number of banner ads placed on your site. The most common rate is 2:1. For every two banner ads on your site, you get a free one on another site. While there are no Irish companies that do this, an example of a banner exchange is LinkExchange (www.linkexchange.com).

PRICING CONFUSION

Currently there is considerable confusion concerning media planning and buying on the Internet. The difference lies in which rate to use:

- *Clickthru rate* is the charge based on the number of people who physically click on the banner ad. It therefore doesn't matter how many people see the ad; only how many click the banner ad and are transported to your site. If no one clicks on the banner ad, you don't pay.

- *Impression-based ads* are charged on the number of people who see the banner ad. The price is regardless of the number of people who physically click on the ad. In other words, even if no one clicks on the ad, you still pay.

There is a difference in pricing methods and it's up to you to find out which is best for your purposes. However, more and more site publishers are opting for impression-based advertising, as this is how traditional advertising prices work and it is easier to understand and explain to potential advertisers.

Publishers don't like clickthru pricing, because if an advertiser designs and constructs a poor quality banner ad, they won't be paid, because very few people click on it. Publishers don't want their income dependent on their clients' inability to design ads. After all, traditional media charges are based on the number of viewers, readers, listeners, etc. who actually see, read or hear the advert. Why shouldn't the Internet be the same? In the years ahead, impression-based pricing should become the norm for Internet advertising.

For some reason, in Ireland many of the large websites charge on a monthly basis. The UK, however, is moving towards the impression-based model. At the time of writing, IOL was charging £500 per month, but was unable to give a clickthru or impression rate. Indigo, 2FM, Clubi likewise are still charging per month. However, more and more sites are using either clickthru or impression-based advertising.

A word of advice: check with site publishers concerning various deals on Internet space. The chances of them selling all their available advertising space are quite low. Often a publisher will sign a deal offering you a below-rate charge if you agree to prepay for a prescribed period of time. However, be careful not to prepay too far in advance — say, more than three months — as sites and publishers have a high failure rate.

Before starting a banner advertising campaign, plan carefully where you're going to advertise your site. Contact some of the banner ad networks in Ireland, the UK, Europe and North America. Be aware, however, that some are disreputable. It is not unheard of that certain networks renege on signed deals because they think they're undercharging you. Also, be warned that many smaller networks are being bought out or are simply going out of business. Check out their sites for their rates and prices, see how they charge and what you'll be receiving from the ad.

Do not sign a contract with them if you do not understand what they're saying or if the contract doesn't say what you want it to say. Make them commit to a deal and, as in all business dealing, read the fine print and have a legal professional check it out before signing.

The next step in your campaign is to figure out how much you can afford to spend on banner ads. Don't use the rent money, or decide to hold off paying Visa as you figure the clickthrus are guaranteed to bring in new customers and orders. Advertising on the Internet is a slow process. Remember that a clickthru of 5 per cent is exceptional. Once you have a budget, stick to it. Don't allow an agency or publisher to talk you into spending more than you can afford.

HOW MUCH SHOULD YOU PAY?

As with any advertising, you should buy as much space as you can realistically afford. As noted earlier, however, how much you pay for the banner ad campaign can be difficult to figure out, as some of your ads will be paid based on CPC, CPM or on a monthly basis. To get to grips with the costs, go to www.safeaudit.com and check out their product called Banner Wizard, which is available for free download from its web site. Banner Wizard is a standalone application that works like a spreadsheet. It calculates in real-time the costs and revenues of a proposed campaign based on information such as expected clickthru rates and net profit per order.

ROTATING BANNER ADS

Another way of purchasing space is a rotating banner ad. This is where your ad is rotated with others on a regular basis. Usually, you share space with five or six other advertisers and when the reader comes in they see one of these ads, depending on when they entered the site. Each site will rotate the ad on the basis of their own software or technical specification. Before agreeing to this, you should ask the site publisher how often the ads rotate, approximately how many people will see the ad, etc. In particular, check the timing of your ad. There's no point in trying to reach a US market if your ad is only visible between 3 a.m. and 5 a.m. Eastern Time (New York Time). To see this in action, check out the inside pages of *The Irish Times* on the web; they use this as a method of advertising.

DESIGNING BANNER ADS

Now that you have picked your sites and decided how much you can afford to spend, you next need to design the banner ad. The first thing you should remember about banner ads is the size. Standard banner ad sizes are 60 pixels high, 460 pixels wide and no more than 8 kilobytes in file size.

You obviously need to design a banner ad that will encourage people to click on it. You must think about the message you want to put across and express it in a simple way, as you don't have a great deal of space to use. Figure 5.1 shows a banner ad for ireland.com.

Figure 5.1: Banner Ad for Ireland.com

There are, however, a few flies in the ointment: some sites will not allow anything more than a company's logo to be the advertisement. Think long and hard before committing to this, as it could be difficult to provide enough information to encourage someone to click on a company logo.

Another way to attract visitors through a banner ad is to hold a competition or have some sort of free offer and to advertise it in the ad. However, some sites will only allow you to use your logo as the ad.

BANNER AD PLACEMENT

Once you've designed your ad, you need to decide whether to place it on a portal site (a heavy traffic site with a large number of links to other sites, e.g. Yahoo, *The Irish Times*) or on an industry-specific site. For example, if you're selling fishing lures, do you advertise on *The Irish Times* in hopes of lots of people seeing your site, or do you advertise on fishing-related sites only? For the latter, fewer people will see your ad, but they will be far more likely to buy your product or service.

This question is important for two reasons. Firstly, you need to know in order to develop your budget to pay for the advertising. Secondly, you need to know for the design of the banner. Obviously what works on *The Irish Times* will not work in the fishing-related sites, and vice versa. *The Irish Times* will also cost considerably more to advertise on than any small fishing-related sites.

You next need to decide who is to provide the required demographic information in order to make a judgement on which campaign to sink your money into. Do you hire an advertising agency — which specialises in understanding Internet demographics to pick the best sites — or do you surf the Internet and try to find them yourself?

The advantages of using an agency is that they understand banner ad placement, design and content development, and they also may be able to buy the space at a lower cost than you would. Of course, they will charge for this service. So it is really a decision based on time. Do you have the time to surf the web, make contact with the site publishers and negotiate a good deal?

TESTING BANNER ADS

Now it's time to see if banner advertising really works. With real-time measurements (instantaneous readership statistics for your site), you should quickly discover if your ad campaign is working. In order to see this, spread your ad over various sites. Within a week, you should be able to see which sites are most effective and if your banners are really attracting people. If you are getting less than a one per cent response, it's not working. If the ads aren't working, you can quickly change them and start from scratch (try and do this with a magazine or billboard campaign!).

If possible, test the banner ad itself. Some media networks allow clients to test various banners for a higher fee. If they allow you to do this, make two or three slight changes to the banner ad and place them on different sites with similar user demographics and see which ones work the best.

BOOKING FEES

Where does all your hard-earned money go when you book your ad? If you have an advertising agency, it will take a 15 per cent or higher fee, the ad network may take another 15 per cent and the remainder goes to the website publisher for actual ad space.

Can you avoid using an ad agency or ad network? Yes, but consider what you are giving up and will have to do to replace their knowledge, time, energy and effort — not to mention their buying power.

An agency or broker may represent several hundred large or small websites and will have them categorised, know all user demographics and the site publisher's record — do they pay, do they truly update on a regular basis, etc. If you do this yourself, be prepared to spend lots of time surfing the web to find user demographics, prices, space availability and other related information. The broker usually has all this information at their fingertips. Some even have exclusive relationships with certain sites — in other words, you can't advertise on those sites unless you go through the broker.

ADVANTAGES OF WEBSITE ADVERTISING

The biggest advantages the web has over traditional advertising are:

- Cost
- Potential readers
- Real-time measurements
- Interactivity
- Depth of information.

Cost

The cost of advertising on the web is a fraction of the cost of advertising in a newspaper or magazine, or on radio or television. The average cost of advertising in the on-line edition of *The Irish Times* for one month is cheaper than taking out a full-page four-colour ad in the business section on a Wednesday. Also, the product costs for Internet-based advertising are cheaper than those involved in developing a traditional ad.

Potential Readers

You have a better chance of reaching a much broader range of potential customers with the web than with traditional advertising. There are over 100 million people world-wide with Internet access, including approximately one million people in the UK and Ireland. And best yet, if you advertise properly, you could reach a vast new market.

Interactivity

As noted earlier, the Internet is truly the world's only interactive medium. How many times have you had a conversation with your TV, or has the Sunday paper asked for your views on something? By using the Internet properly, you can do both and much more.

Depth of Information

The Internet offers a depth of information that is unsurpassed in any other medium. Anything you need to know about any industry, company, product, or market is out there — and your information had better be included!

Information can be layered so that a few clicks take the visitor from novice-level overviews to in-depth specifications. Even the smallest site these days can easily grow to 100 pages.

Imagine what the cost would be to distribute that much information in a traditional medium, like paper. Now imagine how much more information you could be distributing, to take advantage of your site's almost limitless capacity.

THE BOTTOM LINE

The Internet is a new medium and we are still learning how to exploit it. It's hard to grasp because it's so complex — interaction can be both anonymous and communal, information can be both vast and accessible.

New facets of community, technology and the marketplace will continue to emerge. The complexities of a medium that can be one-to-one, one-to-many, and many-to-many — all at once — are just now being revealed.

But remember: the best way to chart any new territory is to simply forget the old models and start exploring.

SELLING SPACE

Now let's look at the flip side of the coin: selling space on your site. The first thing you need to know is how many people come into your site. Traffic figures have to be made available to potential advertisers, or they won't advertise.

Secondly, you need to know the demographics of your traffic. What good is it to say "we had 1 million hits last week" if you don't know where they came from, what pages they looked at, what browser and operating system they're using, etc.

Thirdly, you will have to decide if you are going to be a portal site (Yahoo, *The Irish Times*) or a site targeted only to specific groups or people.

After you have decided these issues, you must then set your price. When first starting out, you will most likely have more ad space in your inventory than you can possibly sell. If this is the case, you may give some space away or below cost in hopes that advertisers will be willing to pay more at a later date. Or you can set your prices and stick to them and not worry about any unsold space.

I would suggest that once you set your price, you should stick with it. It doesn't cost much to leave space blank if you don't have advertising on a page. However, once you start giving people deals, they will constantly be expecting them and while you may be running lots of ads, your server space has increased and bandwidth requirements will also increase, which could cost you more money in the long run. Keep deals for those clients who prepay or are buying lots of space for a few clients, e.g. an advertising agency.

Don't rely on advertising revenue to cover the cost of the website. You must do a lot of work marketing and managing the site before you even consider accepting advertising on it. Advertisers expect a lot of useful information about the site. This all takes time to develop and achieve.

When you are selling space, look for clients who are not in direct competition with you and can offer your readers something useful, someone who enhances your site, has a good reputation and will not hurt your company image. Do you really want to have a reader that you spent so much time and effort attracting to your site click on a link and go directly to your competition? Don't just take on a client for the sake of boosting your advertising revenues. Make sure your readers will get some type of useful and additional information from the site. Try and keep them related to your service.

MEDIA BUYING FAQS

Q. What are the various methods of paying for Internet advertising?

A. In the UK and Ireland, you can pay for ad space in one of three ways: by the number of people who click on your banner ad, the number of people who see your banner ad or on a straight monthly flat fee.

Q. Why are there three different types of banner ad payment?

A. On the Internet, there is as yet no set standard. Some sites allow you to pay on a CPC (cost per clickthru) because they may not yet have achieved high enough reader statistics to charge on a CPM (cost per thousand) or impression-based rate. Or they simply may not know the difference. Monthly rates in Ireland are still used because it is easier for people to understand paying £500 per month for the ad, rather than paying 5 pence per page view/impression or 20 pence per clickthru. Be warned: not many sites outside of Ireland charge a flat monthly rate. Many sites in the UK charge on an impression-based rate, which becoming the norm.

Q. What can I put into a banner ad?

A. To start with, banner ads are usually 460 pixels wide by 60 pixels deep and 8K in size. Other than that, you can put pretty much put what you like into a banner ad. A word of advice: don't promise something you can't deliver. Likewise, don't mislead people by putting into your banner ad something you don't offer.

Q. Why should I use an advertising agency to handle my media buying for me? Can't I do this myself?

A. The best reason for using an agency is time. You can save a lot of time, energy, hassle and money by hiring a specialist agency. They have the rates, the user demographics of the sites, site addresses, contacts and buying power already established with many sites. Otherwise, you have to look up related sites you would like to advertise on, contact them, negotiate a price, design and create the banner ad and finally deliver it to them. Can you do this yourself? It might be cheaper and a better use of your time to have the agency do all this work for you.

Q. What's the difference between an advertising agency and a banner network?

A. An advertising agency will handle all aspects of your advertising campaign, such as media planning and buying, banner design and construction, price negotiation and provision of campaign statistics. A banner network is an organisation that allows sites to swap banner ads so that both can increase traffic. Some networks don't give you any say in where your banner ad appears, or what comes back to your site. Don't worry, you won't be asked to provide space to a direct competitor or an ad not related to your site, i.e. adult material on a child or family-related site. They don't charge, and they do provide the valuable return information you need to know if your advertising campaign is working.

6

MEASURING THE RESULTS:
WHAT DO THEY TELL YOU?

Now that you have your website, have registered it with search engines, developed a marketing and promotional campaign and perhaps even purchased media space, it's time to measure the results of all this hard work and effort to see if really is working.

One way to do this is by reading any feedback that comes to you through the site. However, if no one is providing feedback, you can't measure the results. How can you check the number of people who visited the site, what pages they read, what information, if any, they downloaded? You can't. So a better way to measure site traffic is required.

In the early days of the web — not so long ago — many sites used a simple "hit" counter, thinking this would provide them with the numbers they needed. Yes, a counter will provide you with the number of hits registered on the site. However, you still can't find out specific information concerning your visitors' site usage.

Realistically, the only way to measure results effectively is through analysis of your server's ASCII log file. Log files, their purpose, technology and features, are explored in further detail later.

By looking at your ASCII log's referrer information, you can determine what site a reader was visiting before coming to yours. Armed with this information, you can not only find out who is visiting the site, but you can also measure the success of your search engine registration. For example, if you read the log and discover that most people coming into your site found you in Yahoo, but very few found you using Excite or Alta Vista, you know that you have been successful with Yahoo but will have to work on your placement with Excite and Alta Vista.

You can also measure the results of any affinity marketing (cross-linking) campaigns you may have developed. As with the search engines, you should have a list of exchanged links. By reading the referrer information, you can determine if traffic is coming in from these exchange links. If so, great, keep it up. If not, however, you may want to drop these links and try new ones.

One of the more important aspects of visitor site interaction that an analysis programme will tell you is how the reader actually navigated around your site. If you were to examine where a reader entered and exited your site, you would be surprised how many people come into a page other than the home page first. You would also be surprised where they choose to exit from your site. With this information, you should be able to make changes that will keep them in the site longer or tempt them to visit pages you want them to see, such as products, services, order forms, company information, etc.

These are the main reasons why you should analyse your traffic. Many people are surprised where their traffic is coming from and the way people navigate around the site. Pages that you figured would be popular are not and information you thought would be of no interest proves important.

More specifically, a good analysis package helps you to find out the following:

- How many people have come into your site;

- Which pages they looked at and which ones they didn't;

- What type of browser and computer system they're using;

- What country they're from;

- What errors or broken links are on your site;

- How many files and kilobytes have been downloaded by each reader;

- The date and time they looked at the file;

- How they navigated the site;

- How many unique visitors came to the site;

- How many hits were recorded by the site.

When you combine all of this information with existing customer databases, you should be able to determine if people coming into your site are potential customers or not, what type of information they're looking for and how you can best fill their needs.

In order to obtain this information, you need two things: an ASCII log file and an analysis program. Once you have run your ASCII log file through the program, your results should tell you how successful the site really is. This is known as web mining; that is, the combining, reading and analysing of user statistics and other company databases to find out more information about your visitors. You can obtain a freeware or shareware log analyser at http://www.tucows.com.

For example, you should find out how well your search engine registration and cross-linking programs are working. By reading the referrer page information, you can find out which search engines visitors are coming from, which links are bringing people in and which ones are not. Armed with this information, you can then concentrate on the ones that need additional work and registration. You should also be able to measure any banner ad campaigns you might have undertaken.

Without good analysis programs, finding specific user information could be like looking for a needle in a haystack. A busy website could attract users from all over the world, especially if it is a portal or content rich site — the traffic could be enormous. With a large amount of traffic, the web manager could find it difficult to provide the proper statistics in a readable form.

WHY MEASURE WEB TRAFFIC?

There are a few reasons you should measure and monitor website traffic. Firstly, you can find out how successful your search engine registration has been. By reading the referrer file information, you can determine which sites your visitors were in before coming into yours. This also applies to affinity marketing and advertising campaigns.

Secondly, you can check the quality of users coming into the site. Are they really potential customers or clients, or are they just surfing through your site?

Thirdly, armed with all the user demographic information, you can then optimise your site for the majority of your readers. For example, if you find that the majority of your site visitors are using a Windows 95/98 operating system with a Netscape Browser, you should design your site to be optimised for these users. Also, it will let you know if you can use Java, Java Script (please note, these are not the same language), Dynamic HTML or any other high level programming by seeing what version of the browser most of your visitors are using.

WHAT ARE LOG FILES?

Before measuring and monitoring log results, we should take a look at them and find out what they are. A log file is simply a record of the files (graphic, text or image) that have been downloaded by a visitor to your site. When a visitor enters a site, their browser sends a request to the host server for HTML pages, graphics, images or any other required programs (e.g. cgi or java scripts). While the server processes this information and sends it back to the user's computer, it also logs the files that were requested by the user and records the time and date they were requested, the URL they used to access your page, and the type of operating system and browser visitors used to view your site. All of this information is then stored in an ASCII file. While this is all useful and required for a clear picture of the site user, it can be difficult to interpret all of this data.

You can run all this information through an analyser (a computer programme), which turns the ASCII log file into useful information in chart and graph form, or if you prefer, you can do the work yourself. Be warned, however; analysing all the recorded data yourself is very time-consuming (it could take days or even weeks). This is the reason you need an analysis program.

In order to give you all the necessary information, the analysis program requires four separate statistical packages, listed here in order of importance:

- *Transfer Access Package*: This tracks all file requests made to the server. It then records the time and date of the request, the IP address, the HTTP file and the number of kilobytes downloaded from your site and finally the visitor's IP address.

- *Referrer Log Package*: This records information concerning what site the visitor was at before coming to yours. This is the only way of measuring search engine registration success, cross-linking strategies, advertising campaigns, etc.

- *Agent Log Package*: From this information, you can find out what type of browser and computer operating system a reader is using. The site can then optimise for people using the most popular browser. This is because there is a difference in the way sites look in different browsers. For example, Netscape displays tables and charts slightly differently than Internet Explorer does.

- *Error Log Package*: This records any dropped connections, timeouts, file not found messages, forbidden access and any others errors or broken links found in your site.

WHAT LOG-FILE ANALYSERS DO

Now that we know how analysers examine traffic statistics and collect the required information, let's look at how the program actually works. A log-file analyser takes all the above packages and puts them into easy-to-read graphs and charts to help you understand what is truly happening with your site. Reading an ASCII log file without the aid of an analyser program is difficult and time-consuming. The raw ASCII file could be anywhere up to 50 MB in size (more than ten times the size of most websites). The program can reduce this to a more manageable format. The simplest versions of these programs create nothing more than a "top ten" list of visitor statistics. For example, you'll receive the top ten referrer pages, the top viewed pages of your site, etc.

While each analysis program does essentially the same job, they differ in how they provide the final printout of the information. Some transfer log files to a vendor. Some, however, are only available to view through a special URL address connected to your site; for example, www.yourcompany.ie/results.

ANALYSER FEATURES

Before setting up a log analyser, be careful to make sure you can use the product. Some can only be used on a Unix server, while others can only run on an NT or Windows box. For a list of analysis packages, see www.tucows.com.

Also, make sure the program can access statistics on other servers. This is important if you have separate sites located on different servers. For example, Dell Ireland may have their own site, along with Dell UK, Dell Germany, etc. (see Figures 6.1 and 6.2). To read all of their statistics, they would have to ensure their analyser can access the required information from the separate servers located in each country.

Make sure results can be created in an easy-to-read format or be transferable to a program you know how to use and understand (e.g. Microsoft Access, Excel, Lotus 1-2-3, etc.).

Is it easy to find out where your visitors are coming from by backtracking the IP address? It really doesn't mean much to you if 100 visitors came in from 123.45.67.89. However, it might be more significant if you found out all these people came in from AOL.

Figure 6.1: The Same, But Different — Dell's UK Site . . .

Figure 6.2: . . . Compared with the Irish Site

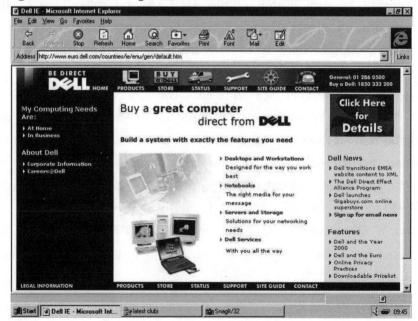

Data Reporting and Analysis

A good analysis program will make it easy for you to read and understand outputs of site-user demographics. From this information, you should be able to determine if the site is successful or not. A good program will enable anyone within the organisation to read the output and make an informed decision on the website.

Extendible and Programmable

As your site grows, so should your analysis package. The best programs allow tools to be added and programmable features to be included as the site progresses. If you buy an analyser that doesn't grow or allow programmability, you may soon have to replace it with a bigger and better one. As with your site, plan it so your analyser can grow in the future.

Cost

One of the biggest considerations is cost. There are freeware (free) and shareware (free for a trial period) analysers. Remember: you do get what you pay for. However, shareware is a good way to try a package before purchasing it. This allows you to see if the program is the right fit for your organisation, without having to lay out a large sum of money.

OTHER METHODS OF TRACKING SITE TRAFFIC

Using Cookies

This is one of the more confusing tools used on the Internet today. Many people are unsure of what exactly a cookie is and what it does. Let's find out what they are, how they work and what their purpose really is.

First off, cookies, developed by Netscape, are not executable programs. Simply put, it is a unique code a server sends to a browser when information is requested. The cookie is then stored on the visitor's hard drive. Don't panic: it takes up a very small amount of computer memory and, unlike Java, it can't affect your hard drive in any way. When the visitor returns to the site, the cookie is activated and records that this person has returned to the site. Amazon.co.uk makes extensive use of cookies.

The advantage of using cookies is that you can track individual site readers entering and returning to your site, allowing you to create a database of site users and their demographics.

However, because people don't really understand what a cookie is and what it does, they may feel they are dangerous, taking up memory space or even reformatting their hard drive (erasing all data stored on your computer). Cookies do not have this capability. The other reason people don't like cookies is that they fear it is an invasion of privacy — i.e. they are being added to an Internet user database. However, this can happen by joining a few newsgroups or discussion groups. It can also happen just by registering your site with a search engine. Lastly, many people don't like cookies because the publisher is storing information on your hard drive without paying for it or compensating you in any way.

If you still don't relish the thought of cookies appearing on your hard disk, don't fear — most browsers allow you to turn the cookies option off.

Data Integration / Web Mining

This involves a lot more work and time to figure out a typical site user profile. This is done by taking your analysed site visitor information and combining it with other company databases (e.g. clients, sales leads). By comparing who is visiting the site against your customer profile, you can easily and quickly discover if the site users match your clients or if they're a new and different group of users.

Browser Optimisation

By cross-comparing all the information a visitor leaves behind them, you should be able to optimise your site: do you need to add special features such as foreign languages, java, etc. This gives you the best way forward for improving the design of your site.

Matching File Names with Page Titles

By giving both your files and page titles the same name (e.g. News), you can compare which pages are being accessed and downloaded on a regular basis. You should also receive information on the date and time the files were accessed.

Navigation Analysis

By sorting each visitor to the site based on the time and date they visited, you should be able to find out the route each person took through your site. This information can then be used to find out which are the most popular pages, which are not, where you should put information to keep them in the site, etc. For example, if you find out that most readers are leaving after the news section, this may be a place to put special offers for Internet users, keeping the reader in your site and encouraging them to look at your product or service and, hopefully, buy.

Converting IP Addresses Back to Web Addresses

As noted before, every website address is really what is called a DNS number, which looks something like 123.45.67.89. The reason for using a name is to make it easier to remember.

Therefore, when a visitor enters http://www.widget.ie into their browser, the DNS system converts this to the appropriate IP address so computers can connect with each other and transfer the requested information. Some good analysis programs will convert these numbers into names. Some will convert most, but not all. However, you can simply go to the address bar in the browser, type in the IP address number and it should take you to the home page of the site and give you the corresponding IP address name.

Data Collection through Packet Sniffing

Packet sniffing technology is one of the latest methods used to measure site performance. The Internet works by breaking down a page into various packets and then sending each packet to the requesting computer via a different route. Some information may be routed through the UK, some through Australia and some through Canada before finally arriving on your machine. You can add what is known as a sniffer to read the packets of information your visitor requests. The advantage of this is the real-time collection of user data. You can immediately discover who is accessing your site. There is no need to store large amounts of data and log files and then analyse the information; you already have it. This technology is really only for organisations with multiple sites. The major disadvantage of packet sniffing is its cost — prices start around £10,000!

RESULTS FAQS

Q. Why should I measure web traffic?

A. Without measuring and monitoring website traffic, you will not know whether your website is successful or a waste of time, energy and money. Furthermore, you won't know which sections of your site are working, which are not, what needs changing and what needs removing. Also, you measure the results of your marketing, promotional and advertising campaigns by checking the referrer data.

Q. What are log files?

A. Log files are ASCII records of website traffic. Every time a browser requests a file (text or graphic), a record of that data is stored in a file. From this information, you can find out who is using the site, what pages they're reading, where they have come from, etc. From this record, you find all sorts of useful information for the management of your website.

Q. What is a log analyser?

A. A log analyser is simply a computer program designed to take the log ASCII file and convert it into charts and graphs. Most ISPs will provide you with some type of log analyser.

Q. What should log analysis tell you?

A. By analysing your log file, you should find the following:

- What country your visitors are from;
- What page they were on before coming to your site, e.g. http://www.yahoo.com;
- What operating system and browser they're using;
- What are the most popular — and least popular — pages;
- What errors and broken links are on your site;
- User demographics.

Q. What is web mining?

A. Web mining is a process where you combine the log analysis data with existing client databases to provide a better understanding of who is coming into the site and why.

Q. Why is web mining useful?

A. From all this data, you can now develop the content of your site to target your audience more accurately. You should be trying to reach the people who will buy your product or service, and this is one of the best ways to get this information.

Q. What is an IP address?

A. An IP address is a series of numbers given to a computer hooked into the Internet. If you have your own address, your site has a unique IP address. It should look something like 173.89.67.54. You are also given your own IP address by your ISP every time you log on to the Internet.

Q. What are Cookies?

A. Cookies are a computer code placed on your hard drive when you visit a site. They're used by site publishers as a way of knowing every time you visit their site. This information is used to understand who is visiting a particular page and why.

7

WEBSITE MANAGEMENT — HOW TO RUN A SUCCESSFUL WEBSITE

In the previous chapters, we have examined what goes into making good content and why this is important. We then looked at the different ways of marketing and promoting your website and finally how to make sense of your results. Now it's time to put everything together to manage your web presence.

Successful website management involves all of the above aspects and more. You must be careful that the site doesn't become too big and lose direction. Like many companies, websites can become big, awkward bureaucracies simply by growing too fast and not finding out what is working and what is not. Prune your website. Don't be afraid to cut and chop dead or non-working branches in the site. Nurture those that do work and spend time bringing them to life. Here are some key points to keep in mind for managing your website:

- The first step in successful web management is to plan, plan, plan. Most websites aren't planned to fail; managers just fail to plan. With Internet technology changing and growing at an incredibly rapid rate, you must plan your web strategy carefully.

- Map out your site. Start at the beginning to see where you are and where you want to go. How can you get there quickly, easily and effortlessly? Just because you can't afford the bells and whistles today doesn't mean you won't be able to afford them in a few months. Technology prices and costs are falling all the time.

- When developing your goals, it's no good to say that you have registered with the search engines, sent out press releases, bought your domain name, and therefore have a successful website. You must be able to define your business goals and what the Internet can do for you. So what if one million people see the site if they don't interact with you and none of them become customers? Set goals that are realistic. Aim to bring in X amount of visitors, leading to Y amount of sales leads, leading to Z amount of sales, etc.

- Use your log files to see how successful your site really is. Remember to set achievable goals and if you don't reach them find out why by using your log files and web mining techniques. Then fix or change the site accordingly.

- Record and analyse how changes to the site affect visitor rates. More specifically, see if these changes adversely affect or increase the number of visitors to the site. See how this compares to site goals — have sales increased, are you getting more feedback from your visitors, are more people asking questions, etc? Even if traffic increases but sales leads do not, is your site still successful? The answer depends on your objectives.

- Frequently check to see which are the most popular pages and why. Is content (e.g. games, graphics, give-aways, etc.) the reason for the traffic increase? Find out why people come to these pages and use this information to bring more traffic to the less popular pages. Don't be afraid to ask questions on your site by doing a survey. If people tell you useful information, add it to your management techniques.

- When making changes to your site, record the number and what changes were made. Don't make too many changes so that you know which ones work and which don't. A complete site redesign won't give you this information.

- Examine your links strategy and how it impacts on site traffic. Check if the high hit pages have outside links driving traffic to your site. See what, if any, traffic is coming to your website through search engines. Find out if news/ discussion group sessions are improving traffic and why. Spend more time on understanding where your traffic comes from and why than on registering and re-registering with search engines.

- One of the hardest things you'll have to do is to keep up with changes on the Internet. Technology is evolving at a high rate of speed. What is leading edge today may become old hat in three to six months. You must know what is happening and why, and how it will affect your website. You must be able to incorporate changes, but not get caught up in the hype. Understand what works for your specific situation.

Below is a list of useful sites that can help with many of the concepts explained in this book on how to manage a successful website. They range from how to get publicity to the latest technology on the web.

Good luck with your website!

- www.searchenginewatch.com — This tracks and records information on the major search engines, with the latest news and happenings concerning engine marketing. A very good resource site for showing you how to deal with the various engines and how to come to grips with meta tags. This site also offers a high quality newsletter on search engines.

- www.iia.ie — This is the site for the Irish Internet Association. It will give you information on the association, useful links and tips for site marketing and promotion.

- www.web-developer.com — Want to know the latest technology and information used by websites? Have a look here. They offer information on HTML and scripting languages such as Java, Perl, etc.

- www.markwelch.com — If you need information on advertising agency and banner networks, this is the site to visit. Mark not only lists most them and gives you up-to-date information; he also rates them and informs about the integrity of the organisation. A real must-read site.

- www.wilsonweb.com — This site covers everything from e-commerce to site technology. Be warned, however: there is a lot of content in the site and browsing through it can consume a large amount of time.

- www.wired.com — The Wired magazine website, giving you all sorts of technology and business information updated on a daily basis.

- www.newslink.org — Provides a complete listing of on-line newspapers and magazines from around the world. A great resource when issuing press releases.

- www.businesswire.com — Get your press release to editors and journalists around the world. However, this service does charge for press release distribution.

- www.liszt.com — Get a list of many of the thousands of mailing lists in existence. A place to register your own or receive tips on how to market and promote your own mailing list.

- www.onelist.com — Want to create a mailing list? Check out this site. It allows you to create your list without the hardware and software expenses.

- www.tucows.com — This is a great site for getting freeware or shareware computer programmes. You'll find everything from HTML editors to imaging programmes to log analysers.

- www.excite.com — One of the Internet's most popular search engines. Also, its database is used to drive a number of other search engines, such as Netscape and AOL Netfind. This is a very important search engine to be in.

- www.yahoo.com – One of the world's most popular sites. It is often mistakenly viewed as a search engine, but it is in fact a directory. As such, it only list approximately 30 per cent of all websites. To get a listing in this directory, you must be approved by a Yahoo editor.

- www.mirago.co.uk — This is an interesting site for UK users. How many times have you used a search engine only to find all their information is US-based? Some search engines have yet to realise there is life outside the US. Mirage provides information for a UK readership.

- www.niceone.com — This directory provides a great list of Irish-related websites. It is updated regularly and has Irish news and information links.

8

CASE STUDIES

Electricity Supply Board
(www.esb.ie)

COMPANY PROFILE

The Electricity Supply Board (ESB) is a statutory corporation in the Republic of Ireland, which was established in 1927 under the Electricity (Supply) Act. In addition to electricity generation, ESB has had the sole responsibility for the management and operation of the transmission and distribution network in the State.

The Electricity Regulation Bill, published by the Minister for Enterprise, Trade and Employment in late 1998, brought an end to ESB's monopoly in the electricity supply market in Ireland. The Bill established an Electricity Regulator and prepared the industry for deregulation. ESB has, however, been preparing for competition for a number of years. One significant aspect of ESB's preparation has been the use of advertising, both traditional and on the Internet, as a means of providing information about the company, increasing ESB brand awareness and reinforcing the importance of ESB in the Irish people's everyday lives.

TRADITIONAL ADVERTISING

As a semi-state organisation with no competition, advertising has not always held the same importance for ESB as for other businesses. With impending deregulation of the market, however, ESB is obliged to place a greater emphasis on branding, consumer awareness and promotion of its services.

The most recent of ESB's advertising campaigns has used the tag line "Where Do They Get Their Energy?" A number of media were exploited, including newspapers, billboards, radio and television.

In 1996, ESB decided to increase brand awareness online via the Internet. A tender was placed and the first ESB website went live in February 1997 at http://www.esb.ie.

INTERNET MARKETING

The original site took its style from ESB brochures and salesware to provide a consistent "look" throughout the company's marketing activities. The site was highly successful and won an inaugural Golden Spider Award for Special Communications in 1997. It also recorded over 30,000 unique visits from users in 86 countries in just 18 months.

The website was completely redesigned and re-launched in August 1998 (see Figure 8.1). In the style of an online magazine, the site is updated every week. Using the robust format of a web-based publication allows the site to increase its level of content regularly, while remaining navigable.

The styling of the site again took its lead from current ESB advertising and printware. The curved frames for images and

headings, the akzidenz font and blue colouring used throughout are in harmony with ESB's offline branding.

Figure 8.1: The ESB Website

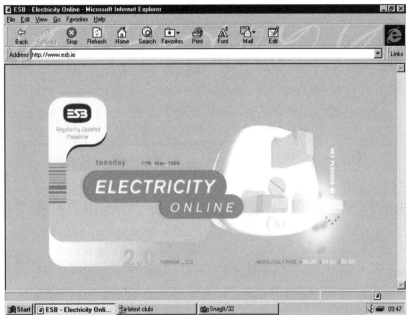

The site not only provides the typical company profile, history
and financial statements, but also includes features on a range
of ESB-related content.

Information on the production of electricity, plant engi-
neering and an ever-growing area of power station mini-sites
are all included in a section called Generation. Twenty-three
ESB power stations and renewable energy projects will have
their own mini-sites, complete with 360° views, QuickTime
movies, history, location and interesting facts. Number 29 — a
renovated Georgian house in Dublin owned and operated by
ESB and the National Museum — also receives its own treat-
ment, giving the visitor a sneak preview of what's in store
when history is brought to life. An Education section includes

interactive experiments and safety information, while the Environment and Customer sections include fisheries details, energy-saving tips and the Customer Charter.

The site is well designed and thought out, with clean and intuitive navigation. One of the best features about the site is its division of content. For example, if you want to learn more about the company, you can read an outline of the Corporate section with one simple click. One more click gives detailed information about the company history, current structure and projects.

The site was designed with a number of factors in mind: ease of navigation, fast download speed and the ability to scale up the site's sections over time with the addition of more content.

The importance of intuitive navigation is manifold. The age and range of the potential ESB website users are wide, from schoolchildren to the elderly. It was therefore very important that a user, perhaps with little Internet experience, could find the information they wanted quickly and easily.

Given the user profile, the site was built to accommodate users with average bandwidth speeds, browsers and machines. The site therefore downloads quickly, does not require plug-ins to view most areas of content, but does offer higher levels of interactivity to users who want it (e.g. DHTML, Live Picture, etc.).

The site was also designed in a way that allowed it to be updated weekly. A user therefore sees new features or articles on the Home Page of the site every time they revisit.

However, just because a site is well designed and easy to navigate doesn't mean visitors will find it. To attract users to the site, ESB have undertaken a campaign of search engine registration, online promotion and online media buying.

SEARCH ENGINE REGISTRATION

ESB has been registered with the major international search engines: Yahoo, Excite, Alta Vista, HotBot, Lycos and Infoseek. Separate meta tags have also been developed for each section of the site. However, ESB needs to develop a quarterly monitoring and re-registration programme for both Irish and international search engines. Meta tags, if they are found to be ineffective, should also be redeveloped and included in the site with the re-registration process.

ONLINE MEDIA BUYING

ESB has bought banner space on a number of popular Irish websites, including *The Irish Times*, Ireland On-line, Indigo and Tinet.

Banner space on these sites gives exposure to a wide range of Irish users, again with the aim of making ESB synonymous with electricity generation in Ireland. As the premier portal site in Ireland, *The Irish Times* has proven to be a particularly successful vehicle for developing online brand awareness. *The Irish Times* is one of Ireland's only two Audit Board Circulation (ABC) audited sites. This means readership figures are checked and independently verified by the same group of people who monitor newspaper and magazine figures. The latest figures show that the portal receives 6.03 million page impressions a month.

PUBLIC RELATIONS CAMPAIGN

ESB also developed an online public relations plan for the launch of Version Two of their site. A range of technology journalists were identified and e-mailed with a press release and password, inviting them to a pre-launch view of the new site.

This enabled ESB to track the journalists who had visited the site and directly target them for coverage.

As the site is updated continuously, ESB's Press Office is afforded the opportunity to distribute press releases about new features on a regular basis.

Editorial coverage is important, as to many readers it appears more credible than bought advertising space. ESB has received good press coverage concerning the latest site developments.

SITE UPDATING

The site's redesign and restructuring in August 1998 allowed content to be highlighted and added weekly on a front page "Features" area. Press releases, sponsorship information, ESB news and events are added to the site on a regular basis. The objective of frequent updating of the site is to keep customers informed of ESB's activities, but also to give users a reason to return to the site. A site with static, never-changing content offers the user no encouragement to revisit.

RECOMMENDATIONS AND CONCLUSIONS

The ESB site has a lot going for it. It is easy to navigate and find information quickly. The site follows good content rules (i.e. it is updated and changed frequently). It is interactive and encourages users to ask questions and make suggestions for the site. Indeed, users' feedback formed the basis of the site's revamp. Overall, a well-constructed and well-run site.

A few marketing and promotional tips for ESB would be to give readers a date when they're going to update. While they do this frequently, it doesn't happen at the beginning, middle and end of the month, but when the information becomes available. It might be better for readers to know when these updates will occur.

Developing an online contest to include schoolchildren is another good promotional concept. For example, a competition about a new way of generating cheap hydroelectricity, or how it is currently developed, etc. could be set for schoolchildren of different ages. Prizes could be awarded for the best ideas and would offer both increases in numbers of users to the site and the opportunity for additional press coverage.

Search engine placement should be monitored and the site re-registered if it falls out of the top 50 listings, as most people will not look beyond the top 50 listings in the results section of the search engine. Meta tags must also be redeveloped along with re-registration to the engine or directory.

Online media buying must continue to play a role in the ESB website advertising campaign. Banner ads are an important factor in this area, as will be pop-up windows and sponsorship of particular sites in the future.

One thing ESB do, as should all sites, is monitor the activity of their website. From their quarterly log reports, they find out who is visiting the site and from which countries. It is also possible to monitor the most popular pages on the site, the amount of time a user spends there, and the operating systems and browsers being used. With this information, ESB can analyse where their site can be improved, which areas should be increased and how well a particular advertising campaign is working. Without this information, ESB would never truly know the extent of the success of their website or online advertising campaign.

Oman Moving and Storage (www.oman.ie)

COMPANY OUTLINE

Oman Moving and Storage Company is an international removal company headquartered in Kill, County Kildare with regional offices in Dublin and Cork. Oman is also part owner of OMNI, a worldwide network of moving companies, and FIDI, an international professional moving association. These organisations ensure (a) the financial stability of their membership; (b) that a high-quality service is provided; and (c) that its members dedicate sufficient resources to organisational development and training.

The company began when Patrick Oman, the managing director, was looking for someone to make deliveries of his restored antiques. Fortunately for him, he couldn't find anyone. He started to make his own deliveries — just himself with one van. Before long, others needed his services, not only for Dublin, but also for the rest of the country. Thus, Oman Moving and Storage was born.

From its modest beginnings in Temple Bar, Oman quickly outgrew the premises and moved to Merchant's Yard, beside the Point Depot, in 1987. Employee numbers have also increased over the years; there are currently 60 employees, and with agents world-wide promoting the company, Oman has grown into a multimillion pound business.

But bringing people to Ireland is not Oman's only business. It also offers removal services to Irish people moving across town, throughout the country or even around the world. Another service sees Oman helping people find schools for children, advising on requirements for people coming to Ireland

and many others ways to make a move to a new country easier (see Figure 8.2).

TRADITIONAL MARKETING

Oman has undertaken traditional marketing methods, including advertising in newspapers, magazines and the Golden Pages. It has also contacted and worked with the human resources departments in some of Ireland's largest corporations. This type of promotion gives Oman a good chance of gaining access to the company and showing the high-level of service it can offer clients and potential clients.

A well-designed company logo and Oman's red and green company colours appear on their trucks, packing materials, staff uniforms and company documentation. Oman also relies on word-of-mouth advertising to gain new clients. This is one of the better ways to secure business, but first you must find clients and keep them.

INTERNET STRATEGY

Paul Coy, Oman's finance director, recognised the importance of the Internet for marketing and communications, and decided to see if the Internet could bring in new business and strengthen the relationship with existing customers. To accomplish this, he developed a website for the company, which went live in early 1997. The site itself, while fairly small, gives information about the company, services offered, etc.

The site is, however, very easy to navigate and the reader can easily find information and services offered by Oman. The overall content of the site is good and gives the reader enough general information to help make an informed decision about Oman. Readers can also ask for a quotation by e-mail if they require it.

Figure 8.2: Oman's Website

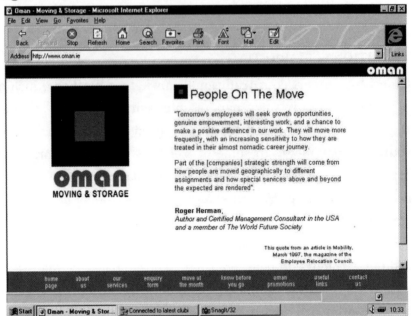

INTERNET MARKETING STRATEGY

Oman registered the site with the search engines, listed site information in brochures and on business cards and company letterheads. However, they quickly learned that this was not enough and are in the process of developing and implementing a new strategy, which is described below.

Re-registering with Search Engines

Oman plans to re-register with all the major international and Irish search engines and to re-develop meta tags to help increase placement in the search engines. Engines they should re-register with are: Alta Vista, Excite, HotBot, Lycos, WebCrawler, Link Star, Galaxy, Infoseek, Yahoo, Search Ireland, Swift Kerna, ieSearch and Nice One.

They have also registered with the Moving Guide, a paid-for link in a database of moving companies. Normally it's not recommended for a company to pay for a link; however, this is a special case in that this directory is marketed directly to people who are looking for a moving company. Also, Oman's competition is listed in the Moving Guide.

Media Buying

Oman has been examining a media buying campaign and considering which is the best route to follow. There are two possibilities for Oman to take. Firstly, it could brand its name by going on high-traffic (portal) sites such as *The Irish Times*. The advantage of this is it would reach a large number of people on a monthly basis. It could also advertise on other high traffic sites such as Go Ireland, etc. The advantage of high traffic sites is simple: some of the large number of visitors to the site will click on the banner ad and enter the Oman site. However, many of these people won't even bother clicking on the Oman logo as they don't require their services.

The second way for Oman to conduct media buying is to look for moving-related sites, government services and large corporate Intranets. This way, they deliver a focused message to people who, on the whole, are more likely to use their service. They can specifically target people or companies who are moving to or from Ireland.

Site Updating

Oman has realised the importance of giving people additional information. They have done this by offering the "Move of the Month" page. This page details a move and all its problems and solutions in a format that is both fun and informative for readers. By offering this, Oman gives a reason for people to return to the site regularly.

Contests

Oman has run a contest for existing clients by mailing out a letter containing a written number and giving readers instruction on how to see if they have won a prize by visiting the Oman website. The result of the competition was an increase in site traffic and a reminder to people that they can communicate with the company via Internet i.e. e-mail, or obtain services and information from the site.

Site Monitoring

Oman monitor their site frequently. After all, why go to all the trouble of marketing the site and giving away prizes if they don't know who is visiting the site and why?

Site monitoring activities include ASCII log file research, which allows Oman to discover who is coming to the site, what site they're coming from, what country they're in, what pages they're reading, what type of computer system and browser they're using to view the site, and so on.

From all this information, Oman can determine what changes they should make, what computer and browser they should optimise the site for, etc. It also helps them to know whether the majority of site readers will be able to use Java, Dynamic HTML and other newer high-level technology. In addition, it lets them know how to make the site user-friendly, enjoyable and informative for the majority of readers.

RECOMMENDATIONS AND CONCLUSION FOR OMAN

Oman have the beginnings of a good, solid practical site. However, they do need to work on it by adding additional informative sections to keep readers coming back for more. For example, they should examine the site and try to give out additional information to prospective clients concerning moving.

They need to keep an eye on search engine placement. They should be monitoring engine placement and results in both the major and Irish search engines and directories at least quarterly. If they fall out of the top 50 listings, Oman should re-register and redevelop meta tags for the engines they have been lost in. Most search engine users will not look past the first three or four pages.

For media buying, Oman should continue looking for both high traffic and niche market ad space. In order to do this successfully, Oman should look at a few high traffic sites such as *The Irish Times* or a high volume moving site. However, this doesn't mean they should stop advertising with smaller moving-related sites, government sites or even Intranet sites. Media buying should be an ongoing project examined frequently to see how well it is working.

As Oman is gearing up to take the site to the next level, web monitoring services are a must. They need to discover if media buying is successful, what search engines most readers are coming from, etc. This will let Oman know if they're spending money correctly or, if they need to change focus, how to change that focus quickly.

Another way of marketing themselves to the Internet community is through news/discussion groups. By offering advice to readers on moving and storage and coming to Ireland (what to expect, etc.) they could bring in new clients for some or all of their services. Such discussion groups (e.g. alt.local and alt.transfer) are available through most ISPs.

Newsgroups seem to be almost forgotten in Ireland when marketing a site. By signing its postings with its website address and e-mail address, Oman could promote its services to a new group of people who are actively interested in moving or the topic of moving. Not all people who surf the web are actively seeking information on moving, but those going to a moving newsgroup are.

Oman could consider using questionnaires and surveys about service and what people would like to be offered by Oman. For example, the company may find, by using a survey, that most clients want to know the requirements for moving to Ireland, or whether Oman can help with specific tasks not usually offered through moving companies (e.g. recommending a good immigration lawyer). They could also offer an FAQ section to answer questions and concerns that clients might have about moving.

Oman should look for ways to involve readers in the site and encourage questions. Readers tend to be receptive to a site where they not only find information, but also become part of the site through conversation. And the Internet is one of the few media that allows this to take place.

Angel Design (www.angel.ie)

Angel Design is a graphics consultancy firm for both the Internet and traditional media. Angel creates and designs brochures, corporate identities, logos, manuals, proposals, web pages, promotional literature, newspaper and magazine advertisements and other related materials. Angel strongly believes that the web will eventually make up 30 per cent of all its business.

Angel realised that developing a website would enable them to market their services to a world-wide audience. However, they also understood that marketing was becoming increasingly necessary to attract people to a website. "Getting our site found has involved more than just registering with a few search engines and waiting for readers to find us," explains Angel's Creative Director Philip Darling. "We decided to make a budget available to bring traffic to us."

As one of the first design groups to go online, Angel has benefited by getting responses from potential clients from both Ireland and abroad. "While it may not have directly brought in new business, it has helped us obtain website work from existing clients and has put the Angel name into the public domain," says Mr Darling. "We've had people from the US, Canada, the UK, the Far East and other parts of Europe ask us for quotes. Under traditional advertising methods, we just couldn't generate leads from these countries."

SITE CONSTRUCTION AND DESIGN

The Angel site contains information about the company and its services. It has an interesting section on angels, including film and book reviews, etc., in order to give readers a fun, entertaining section. The content has gone through extensive changes to offer readers insight into the company (see Figure 8.3).

Angel has also added an extranet section to the website, which allows a private area for each individual client. The purpose of this area is to allow the client to have an initial look at some design work created for them. Clients can then e-mail changes back to Angel, which cuts down on both time and cost involved in having the initial design approved by the client.

Figure 8.3: Angel Design's Website

SEARCH ENGINE REGISTRATION/MONITORING AND META TAG DEVELOPMENT

Unlike many sites, Angel follows up the standard registration process by monitoring engine placement on a quarterly basis. Most people believe that if you have registered with a search once, that is all you need to do but, as the analysis in this book has shown, a lot more is needed.

To help bring traffic to the Angel site, the URL has been registered with the following UK, Irish and international search engines and directories:

- *UK and Irish*: Mirago, Nice One, Swift Kerna, ieSearch and Search Ireland;

- *International*: Excite, Lycos, HotBot, Link Star, Infoseek, Yahoo and Galaxy.

To help increase search engine placement, Angel has developed meta tags for the site. Angel has also developed a philosophy of changing and recreating its meta tags when re-registering with the search engines. Remember to keep meta tags somewhat different from your competitors'. If you don't, there will be no difference in placement between your site and theirs.

This is one of the few sites in Ireland to have used Alternative Text (alt text) tags with their images. Alt text tags serve two functions. Firstly, they help with search engine placement. Secondly, some people surf the web with autoload images off. This enables them to download pages and information more quickly. Without alt text tags, these people would have no idea what image you have placed on the website.

The overall spending on search engine registration and monitoring is approximately 10–15 per cent of the complete budget and it brings in almost 50 per cent of Angel's traffic. This area therefore gives a good rate of return on the investment.

SITE MANAGEMENT

Angel quickly released that while it was beneficial to offer people information about their services and even go so far as to provide additional sections about "Angels" and "Having Fun", they still needed a way to bring readers back to the site. The best way to do this, it was decided, was to offer an updated news and information section to the site.

This section could offer information on what was happening with Angel Design, any new work, or company awards or achievements. Anything that could possibly be of interest to the reader could be placed in this section and revised as necessary. Studies have shown that readers generally must visit a site about three times before they will buy from you. To do this, your site must change in some way and change frequently. After all, once you have seen the site, there is no reason to come back if hasn't been altered.

The other section that is updated and monitored frequently is the client section. Angel clients include a number of large Irish companies such as Farrell Grant Sparks, University College Dublin and Butterworths Legal Publishers. They also count international companies such IBM and Ernst & Young among their clientele.

The client section offers the reader information on the work undertaken by Angel. It shows some examples of this work and lets the reader gain a better understanding of what exactly Angel can do for them.

While site updating is not directly responsible for bringing traffic to the site, it does help bring readers back on a regular basis. For Angel, the cost of site updating is about 20 per cent of the overall Internet budget.

SITE MONITORING

Angel actively involves staff in monitoring site activity in order to find out more about their visitors.

By finding out what computer system and browser Angel's readers are using, they can optimise the site accordingly. Page layouts can then be made for the majority of site readers.

Site monitoring costs Angel approximately 20 per cent of the overall budget, but gives them a great deal of insight into who is using the site, how they're using it and what Angel can do to improve it.

CONTESTS

This is an area where Angel believes it can attract existing clients to its website. The benefits of running a competition are to remind the reader of Angel's services and its continually growing client list, and to impart a message that it also offers web services such as the design of web pages.

To date Angel has run one contest offering clients a chance to win a dinner for two at Eden Restaurant. The contest worked as follows: Angel mailed out a card with a unique number to all its clients. Each client was then asked to log on to the Angel website and see if their number matched with one that was placed on the site. If it matched, they won. Response to the contest was good. And the site received new hits, as people had to visit in order to check their number and return again to see who had won.

The cost for the contest was approximately one to two per cent of the overall budget. However, it encouraged clients to visit the site. One suggestion for their next contest could be to ask the reader to find something hidden in the site. Instead of simply clicking on one page to check out a number, this would encourage users to browse throughout the entire site, reading more and more information about the company.

RECOMMENDATIONS AND CONCLUSIONS

Angel has a good solid understanding of how to market and manage a successful website. They have registered with and are monitoring search engines placement. They have used alt text tags, something that very few sites do. They've offered readers contests and other types of information.

Angel should look at developing a contest for non-clients. This would give them a reason to participate in and come back to the site. It would also keep the company's name in front of new clients.

Angel should also consider giving design hints for users of the web. For example, images should be scanned at 72 dpi instead of 300, as computer screens can only replicate images at 72 dpi. Also, it will take more time to download a 300 dpi image than a 72 dpi one.

Angel should look at participating in both news and discussion groups concerning both web and traditional design techniques. This would distribute their contact information and website address to a specific group of people who are interested in graphic design.

Overall, the site is well constructed. Its navigation is very straightforward. One aspect that should be changed is the addition of a news link to the main row buttons running across each page. This would enable people to access the news page quickly without first having to visit the Info page.

Heritage Irish Crystal (www.heritagecrystal.com)

Heritage Irish Crystal is a brand name owned by Waterford-based Sculpted Crystal. Founded in 1989 by Joe Williams after he left Waterford Crystal, Sculpted Crystal went on to develop and manufacture 33 per cent lead, all mouth-blown and hand-cut crystal products.

In 1990, the Heritage Irish Crystal brand name was developed as a way to bring some of Sculpted Crystal's products to the market under one umbrella. Heritage has also opened a retail shop along The Quay in Waterford City. Over the years, Heritage Irish Crystal has become a family-run business, with Joe as Chairman and CEO, Sonia Williams as Marketing Director, Brian Williams as Production Director and Joe Williams Jr as Master Glass Maker.

In early 1996, Heritage Irish Crystal was looking for a way to increase export sales to the US, the UK and the rest of Europe. An Internet strategy was developed as a way of offering Heritage's range of products including giftware, lighting, collectibles and stemware, to a wider market. However, just creating a web presence was not enough and the site had to be marketed and managed in order to be successful.

SITE CONSTRUCTION

The site was constructed to allow readers to gain an insight into both the company and the products it offers (see Figure 8.4). Readers can enter the site and view a static page of products by clicking on the view products page and then clicking on one of the images signifying one of the four various product types. Or, if preferred, the reader can click on the search section and search the catalogue according to product type (e.g. vase, bowl, stemware, etc.); product cut style (of which they are four: Cathedral, Shannon, Galaxy and Cricklewood); and finally a search can be done on price ranges.

The site also gives background detail on how Heritage Irish makes its products. Readers can gain a basic understanding of how products are blown and then cut into shape with the diamond-tipped cutting wheels. It also informs the reader of how crystal glass is manufactured in bulk form before being made into trophies, glasses or delicate chandeliers.

Figure 8.4: Heritage Irish Crystal's Website

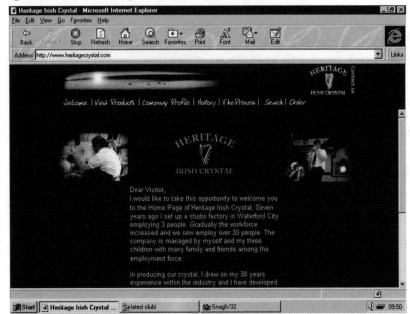

TRADITIONAL MARKETING

Heritage Irish Crystal markets its products by mail order and through a retail outlet. Sculpted Crystal also manufactures products for other companies such as Deise Crystal.

Through mail order and the retail outlet, the market had primarily been tourists visiting Ireland and local people looking for a gift, team style trophy, etc. Mail order business to the US had increased steadily year by year. However, it was decided that the Internet, combined with mail services, could increase brand awareness and ultimately sales of Heritage Irish Crystal's products to people worldwide.

SITE MARKETING

Search Engine Registration

Heritage Irish Crystal has registered with the following UK, Irish and international search engines:

- *UK and Irish*: Mirago, Nice One, Swift Kerna, Search Ireland and ieSearch.

- *International*: Lycos, HotBot, Excite, Yahoo, Alta Vista, Link Star, Galaxy, Webcrawler, MetaCrawler, AOL Netfind, Infoseek and Inkatomi and various shopping malls and Irish-related sites (see below).

Monitoring of engine placement and re-registration, if necessary, is completed on a quarterly basis.

Shopping Mall Registration

There are numerous shopping areas being developed for the Internet. Shopping malls and other types of related sites are emerging all the time. Some you can register with for free and some must be paid for. Prices vary from mall to mall; some can be very good value, while some can be as high as US$1,000 per quarter. Check with each shopping site to see if they charge. Look for the free ones, as shopping malls are still not the traffic providers people thought they would be. None of the thousands of shopping malls are in the top 25 highest used sites on the Internet.

Heritage has registered with various shopping-related sites (Ireland On-line's Best of Ireland Shopping; Indigo's Highstreet; E-Jay Shopping; Yahoo Shopping; Excite Shopping) and constantly changes the registration as pricing and traffic statistics determine if staying registered with the site is of benefit to them. If a shopping mall is not bringing in at least 25,000 unique visitors per month, it's not worth registering with.

Irish Interest Sites

There are a plethora of Irish-related websites. They range from sites looking at history to the conflict in Northern Ireland to shopping sites, tourist sites and family heritage sites (e.g. All Things Irish; Mining Company — Ireland; Celtic Links). With so much interest in anything Irish, these (usually US-based) lists can bring traffic to a site because it is Irish and has something to say.

Cross-Linking Strategy Development

This happens when related but non-competitive sites exchange HTML-coded links with each other. The advantages of exchanging links are that many people remember how to find to a website by visiting one they know and then linking to the one they want. You can bring new traffic to your site which otherwise may not know you exist.

However, you should be warned to verify and research sites before linking with them, as you could end up of a site that is of no use or otherwise detrimental to your own site. Heritage Irish Crystal has an ongoing linking policy with flatware manufacturers and china makers, etc.

Media Buying

This is buying physical site space from a high-traffic (portal) website. Heritage Irish Crystal examined various high-traffic and shopping-related sites and found that *The Irish Times* would generate some of the best traffic for them.

Heritage Irish Crystal purchased their rotating banner which would appear to just under 1 million readers. This has helped increase both Irish and international traffic to the site. Heritage will continue to look at other portal (high traffic) and Irish and shopping-related sites for future media buying activities. They will only purchase if the return on investment is warranted.

What's New Announcements

As the site has only recently gone live (late 1998), Heritage Irish Crystal can take advantage of the "What's New to the Internet" announcement lists for the next few months. This could bring them a few more visitors.

Site Review Submission

Heritage has also submitted the site for review to site reviewers and journalists in order to hear their ideas on possible changes. Some of the reviews may give them a rating; even a mention that the site exists should create more traffic.

Site Monitoring Activities

Heritage Irish Crystal monitors engine placement quarterly. They re-register the URL if the site falls from the top 50 entries.

Traffic Monitoring

Site visitors are also monitored on a monthly basis. By examining the ASCII log, Heritage can find out who has visited their site, when, what they read, where they're from and what site they were at before entering heritagecrystal.com. This is important so they can justify the expense and time used in constructing and marketing the site.

Web Mining

By combining already existing client profiles with website user demographics coming from the ASCII log file, web mining can give Heritage Irish Crystal a better look at who is coming into the site and how to sell to these visitors.

Site Updates

Heritage has the ability to update the site when it adds new products to the line. By adding the new information into the site database, it can be updated along with company catalogues and marketing information. This is important so that both company literature and the website grow and change at the same rate.

RECOMMENDATIONS AND CONCLUSION

Heritage Irish Crystal, like Angel, has decided that search engine registration is something that must be done in order to have a successful website. They also realise that they must monitor their placement and re-register when necessary.

Heritage Crystal has undertaken a large number of marketing activities designed to bring traffic and eventually sales to the site. It should be one of the more successful websites in terms of traffic and sales, if this marketing programme is carried out. However, another thing they could do is to join discussion/news groups and mailing lists to offer their advice on retailing via the web (e-commerce) and crystal manufacturing, exporting products or even just manufacturing. They could sign all their postings with their name, e-mail address and site address, which encourages people to come to their site.

They're also practising what is known as web mining, which is something very few companies actually perform. While it will cost money to do, mining and monitoring will give them insight into site traffic which most organisations don't have.

Another recommendation is for Heritage Irish Crystal to undertake additional media buying services. This way, traffic coming to the site should increase. Also, it is a cost-effective branding method and, since Heritage Irish Crystal is a brand name, it should be developed and the Internet is the best way for this to happen. Also, by undertaking additional media buying activities, they can further increase their branding campaign at a fraction of traditional advertising costs.

Examples of
Other Successful Websites

Figure 8.5: Finfacts — http://www.finfacts.com

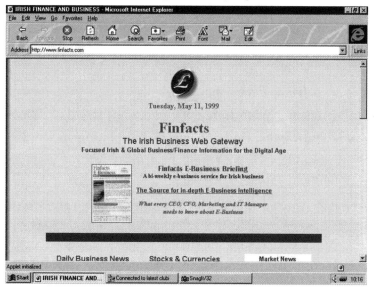

This is an Irish-based business and financial site. If you're looking for business news, highlights or financial news and information concerning Ireland, this is an excellent site. It is easy to navigate; it has a Yahoo-style front end and contains links and original content, making it easy to understand and surf. *Rating: 8 out of 10.*

Figure 8.6: Ireland.com — http://www.ireland.com

This is *The Irish Times'* new portal site for Irish-based sites and information. From here, you can read the daily electronic edition of the *Times*, find out what's happening in Dublin with a live event guide, or link to other Irish sites. *Rating: 7 out of 10.*

Figure 8.7: Amazon.co.uk — http://www.amazon.co.uk

The UK version of the world famous Amazon.com site. While Amazon have yet to make any money from the Internet site (figures show the company losing $10 million per quarter), the site is still one of the best retail sites available. By using cookies an other technology, they know when a user returns, and this allows them to tailor the site for each individual reader and help them find what they are looking for quickly and easily. *Rating: 9 out of 10.*

Figure 8.8: Wired — http://www.wired.com

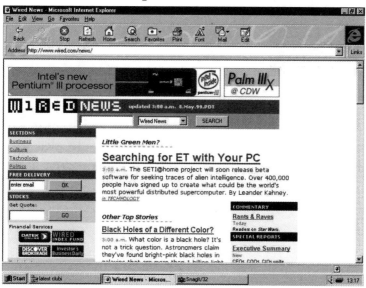

This is Wired Magazine's Internet site. One of the first truly informative and useful sites on the Internet. Wired covers breaking, business, technology, cult and promotional news. They offer information on how to design, create and market a site through Web Monkey. *Rating: 9 out of 10.*

Figure 8.9: Dell Computers — http://www.dell.co.uk or http://www.dell.ie (for Irish readers)

Dell is one of the few retail success stories on the web. The site allows readers to order online. It's very easy to pick the computer and peripherals required. *Rating: 8 out of 10.*

GLOSSARY

A lot of different concepts have been explained through this book. Some are old hat, such as marketing and promotion (although they are explained here in terms of the Internet); however, you may be less familiar with others, such as media buying and web mining. This glossary reviews some of the terms we used. *(Words in italics are to be found elsewhere in this glossary.)*

Advertising Agency — A company specialising in the marketing and promoting of a *website* by advertising it in various media.

Affinity Marketing — The exchange of *hypertext links* with a related but non-competitive *website*; for example, a crystal manufacturer exchanging links with a china company.

ALT Tags — Imbedded *HTML* tags used to describe an image, to allow the *search engine* to read what the image is and therefore help improve placement results. Also to allow those who surf the *Internet* with the autoload images option turned off to have an idea of what the *graphic* might be. (Switching off autoload images allows for quicker page download.)

ASCII — A standard code used by all computers to change numbers, punctuation marks and signs into corresponding letters so that a user can understand and read what is on their computer screen.

Banner Ad — A *graphic* constructed to attract a reader's attention to encourage them to click on it and be transferred to the advertiser's website.

Banner Ad Network — An organisation that helps in the buying, selling and construction of a *banner ad*.

Banner Exchange Service — An organisation that helps people exchange *banner ad* space, often for free. However, this usually works on a ratio of 2:1. For every banner ad that is placed, a publisher must put two on their *website*.

Browser — Computer software that converts *HTML* code into something a user can see and read. The two main browsers in use are Netscape Navigator and Microsoft Internet Explorer. There are also different versions of the browsers.

CGI (Common Gateway Interface) — Contrary to popular belief, CGI is not a program. It is a computer protocol used to define the ways information can be sent from a *server* to a visitor's *browser* and vice versa.

Click — When a user clicks the mouse button on their computer.

Click Rate — The number of times someone presses their mouse button to enter or leave a *website*.

Content — The material that goes into making a *website*. It includes text files, *graphics*, images, line drawings — whatever appears on the page is content.

Content Rich Site — A *website* that relies on unique *content* as its method of bringing in readers. Any of the major daily newspapers are content rich sites.

Cookies — Following the strange tradition of naming *Internet* functions after food (*spam*, cracker), cookies are small programs, invented by Netscape, unobtrusive little bits of information that slip onto a hard drive, essentially without the user's knowledge, and track where they've been and what they've done on a particular *website*. Cookies are useful when it comes to sites that require registration (the cookie stores the user's data so they don't have to remember yet another password) or with configurable sites (the cookie is used to keep track of what interests the user most so the site can present that information first).

CPC (Cost Per Clickthru) — A pre-agreed price between an advertiser and a *site publisher* in which the advertiser is charged every time a user *clicks* on a *banner ad* taking them directly to the advertiser's site.

CPM (Cost Per Thousand) — A pricing method used in media buying based on the number of people who physically see a *banner ad*.

Cross-linking — An exchange of *hypertext links* with related but non-competitive *websites*; for example, a crystal manufacturer may exchange links with a china maker. Also known as *affinity marketing*.

Cross-platform — The ability for a program or *website* to be used, seen or executed on two or more of the different *operating systems*. The *Internet* itself is cross-platform, allowing people to view a site on a Windows, Unix, DOS or Mac operating system.

Data Mining — The analysis of various sources of information; for example, the examination of clients' demographic data in order to get a better picture of who they are and their buying habits.

Database — A computer program used to hold vast amounts of information.

Dial-up Access — The most popular method of connecting to the *Internet*. The user connects their modem to a typical (analogue) phone line, dials the number for their *ISP* and goes online. This is usually the cheapest way of getting Internet access.

Directory — Similar to a *search engine*, in that it is a listing of various *website* addresses available on the web. Like an engine, its database of *URLs* is searchable. Unlike a search engine, it does not travel the *web* looking for URLs to add to its database. The best example of a directory is Yahoo.

Discussion Group — A part of a *website* where readers can go to talk about a subject.

Domain — A category of the Internet with addresses or *domain names* sharing a common suffix such as that standing for a particular country or used by a particular group of users.

Domain Name — A unique name given to a *website* which corresponds to a series of numbers known as an *IP address* used to direct traffic to a site. Could be something like www.mycompany.ie.

Editorial — The written copy used to describe a product or service.

E-mail — Messages distributed by electronic means from one computer to one or more recipients via a network.

Frame — A page construction used in a *website*. Two or more pages are combined to create a single page of information. This is used when the *web developer* requires one or more sections of the page to change, while others remain constant.

Freeware — A computer program made available to an end-user for free. Primarily available via the *Internet* and on CD-ROM formats.

Graphic — An image, photograph or scan created on or stored in a computer program for inclusion on a *website*.

Hit — An old system of measuring visitors to a *website*. Every time a file is requested for downloading from a site, it counts as one hit. Pages contain multiple files and each time a file is requested, a hit is counted.

HTML — Hypertext Markup Language; the code used to create *websites*.

HTTP — Hyptertext Transfer Protocol; the method used to transfer files from a *web server* to a *browser*.

Hypertext Link — A *HTML* link that transfers the user to another section of a specific document or *website* or to another website or place on the *Internet*.

Impressions/Page View — This is a measurement of *website* visitors. Page view examines the number of times an entire page (not just a file) was downloaded by a user.

Internet — A collection of computers linked together for the purpose of exchanging information with each other. Consists of *newsgroups*, *e-mail* and the *World Wide Web*.

Inverted Pyramid Style — A form of writing that should be used when developing *editorial content* for a *website*.

IP Address — A series of numbers given to a computer linked to the *Internet* (for example, 178.345.98.67). A computer is given its own IP address only when the user logs online.

ISDN — Integrated Services Digital Network; high-speed digital access to the *Internet*. Like a *dial-up* account, ISDN uses a modem (in this case a special ISDN modem and digital phone are required) to dial the telephone number provided by an *ISP* and surf the *Internet*. It is very similar to the ordinary dial-up account, but the advantage is the speed with which information can be downloaded.

ISP —Internet Service Provider; a company that provides access to the *Internet* by way of *dial-up* connection, *ISDN* line or *leased line* (24-hour access).

Java — A *cross-platform* programming language developed by Sun Microsystems; uses classes and subsets to perform tasks using a small amount of memory and therefore download time.

Java Script — A small executable program used to enhance a *website's graphics* capabilities. For example, it will add scrolling text to a site, fade background colours and various other tasks. Not to be confused with *Java*.

Keyword — A descriptive word used to describe a *website* to *search engines*. It is included among the *meta tags*.

Leased Line — Another form of *Internet* access, this provides an organisation with 24-hour Internet access, without having to dial the service provider's telephone number. The main disadvantage to this method is the cost. It's very expensive to operate, as the computer is online 24 hours a day, 7 days a week. Companies should think long and hard about using this sort of access before installing it.

List Manager — The person responsible for a *mailing list*. Also called a moderator.

Log Analyser — A software program used to convert *ASCII log files* into data that can be easily read and used to identify site traffic.

Mail Server — A computer housed with an *ISP* for the storage and retrieval of *e-mail*.

Mailing List — A group of like-minded people who discuss a specific topic using *e-mail*.

Meta Tags — A hidden list of *keywords* imbedded in the *HTML* code of a *website* to improve *search engine* result rankings.

Moderated List — A *mailing list* that is managed by a person or people.

Moderator — The manager or person responsible for a *newsgroup*, *discussion group* or *mailing list* (see *list manager*).

News Server — A computer run by an *ISP* that is programmed to read the various *newsgroups* it has subscribed to and made available to clients.

Newsgroup — A group of like-minded individuals who come together to discuss a specific topic. This is primarily done by using the *ISP*'s *news server*.

NT — An *operating system* developed by Microsoft. Used primarily as network *server*.

Operating System — A program used to make a computer work. On the *Internet*, most servers use either NT or Unix; a few use Mac.

Perl — Practical Extraction and Report Language; developed by Larry Wall, it is a *cross-platform* program used for text manipulation. It is the programme most often used in the development of interactive forms, as it can easily break down and extract information so that the user can read it.

Pop Ups — When a new *browser* window pops up. Primarily used for ads or for taking users to another *website*. This method for ads is slowly falling into disfavour, as more and more people object to being transferred from a website when they don't want to be.

Portal Site — Usually a high *traffic* site containing *hypertext links* to other *websites*. It can be related to a specific subject (e.g. Irish-related issues) or not. The best example of a portal site is Yahoo.

Search Engine — A computer program that crawls the *web* looking for and adding new *websites* to its searchable *database*.

Server — A computer hooked directly into the *Internet* to host *websites*, *newsgroups* or *e-mail*, each of which has its own separate server. An *ISP* will have a *web server* used to host *World Wide Web* sites, a *news server* used to host newsgroups and an e-mail server used to hold e-mail.

Server Log File — A file, usually *ASCII*, created by the *web server* to record all the files requested by various visitors to a *website*.

Shareware — A computer program that is free to use on a trial basis, as a way of marketing the product. Developers hope that by giving users a taste of the program, they will learn to use and like it.

Site Hosting — When an *ISP* houses a *website* on its *server* so that it is constantly made available to users.

Site Management — The running and developing of a *website*.

Site Publisher — The person, group or organisation who owns the *website*.

Spider/Crawler — Part of the *search engine* that travels the *web* looking for *websites* to add to a searchable *database*.

Submission Programmes — These are used to register a *website* with various *search engines*. By filling out a form, users are automatically registered with various search engines and *directories*. Submission programmes do not monitor or re-register websites on a regular basis.

Traffic — The active collection of users visiting a *website*.

UNIX — An *operating system* used for *servers* hooked to the *web*. It has gained popularity because of its price — free.

Unmoderated List — A *mailing list* that allows a user to post without having their material vetted.

URL — Universal Resource Locator; a *web address* that is unique to a *website*.

User — A person who surfs the *web* or visits a *website*.

Web — see *World Wide Web*.

Web Address — Commonly known as site address, *domain name* or *URL*. It is in fact the name of the *server* and domain combined to make it unique. For example, www.arcticadv.com is my company's web address. The server name is arcticadv and the domain name is .com.

Web Developer/House — A company or person who creates and constructs *websites*.

Web Manager/Webmaster — The person who is responsible for maintaining the *website*.

Web Mining — Correlating *server log files* with company *databases* to gain a better understanding of who is visiting a website and what data they're downloading.

Web Page — A single document/section on a *website*.

Website — A collection of *web pages* put together to form a single interconnected entity containing information on a company, or its products or services.

World Wide Web — The entire collection of interlinked websites on the Internet.

WWW — see *World Wide Web*.

REFERENCES

Research and information was obtained from the following websites and individuals.

Websites

http://www.forrester.com
http://hotwired.com/webmonkey
http://www.iia.ie
http://www.jup.com
http://www.markwelch.com
http://www.nua.com
http://www.searchenginewatch.com
http://www.submit-it.com
http://www.virtualpromote.com
http://wilsonweb.com
http://www.wired.com

Articles on the Internet

Braitman, Larry, "Crunching the Numbers: Using Banner Ad Testing to get the most out of your Advertising Dollar", *Click Z* (10/6/98)

Busch, David P., "Counting Your Blessings", *Internet World* (6/1/97)

Dugan, Tim, "Avoid the Banner Bugaloo . . . Or Do Your Research", *Click Z* (9/1/98)

DuPre, Cathy, "Getting Better Search Engine Placement", *Internet Information Scavenger* (28/4/98)

Fischler, Michael, "Web Marketers . . . Start Your Engines!", *Click Z* (10/6/98)

Fleischman, Glenn, "Web Log Analysis: Who's Doing What", *Web Developer* (5/1/98)

Gehamn, Joel, "Search Engine Optimisation: Half Art, Half Science, or Half Baked?" *Click Z* (11/10/98)

Greene, William, "Direct Marketing Online", *Submit-it Traffic Tribune* (9/1/98)

Hamilton, Annette, "Biggest Traffic Boost Trick you are Throwing Away", *ZDNet Anchor Desk* (15/7/98)

Heerenzia, Angela, "Is your Website Cart before your Keyword Horse?", *ChannelSeven*

Lang, Paul, "Great Expectations for Banner Ads" *Click Zcommerce* (9/8/98)

Longcrier, Kenneth Joe, "Search Engines", *Search Engine Monitor*

Marketwave Corporation, "Web Marketing", *White Paper* (5/12/98)

Oakes, Chris, ""Does Yahoo Still Yahoo?", *Wired News* (2/11/98)

Smith, Larry, "Viewpoint Comparison on Web Measurements", *Advertising Age* (14/9/98)

Strom, David, "Become a Meta Master", *Windows Sources* (2/1/98)

Sullivan, Danny, "Search Engine Optimisation: The Science and the Art", *Click Z* (11/9/98)

Sullivan, Danny, "Spider Spotting Chart", *Search Engine Watch*

Sweet, Lisa, "Measuring Your Hits", *ZD Internet* (8/3/98)

Taggart, Stewart, "Olympic Data Crunching", *Wired News* (8/3/98)

Traynor, Ian, "Understanding Your Website Visitors", *Affiliates Programmes*

Wilson, Jim, "Understanding Website Traffic Analysis", *Virtual Promote* (30/11/98)

Winnet, Bill, "Tracking Your Visitors", *Hot Wired* (4/12/98)

Non-Internet Sources

Bennion, Jackie (1998), "Go Big or Stay Home", *Wired*, September.

Clancy, Niall (1998), "Speak Out: Promoting Your Web Site On-Line", *dot.ie*, October.

Fox, Ian and Iskandar Abdullah (1995), "The Advertising Agency — Function and Direction", in Tony Meenaghan and Paul O'Sullivan (eds.), *Marketing Communications in Ireland*, Dublin: Oak Tree Press.

Geirland, John (1996), "Go with the Flow", *Wired*, September.

Godsil, Jillian E. (1999), "Exposing Your Site", *Web Ireland*, 24 February to 24 March.

Pratchett, Craig and Matthew Wright (1998), *CGI Perl Cookbook*, London: John Wiley and Sons Ltd.